St. Louis
FIRE STATIONS

Robert Pauly
with Dennis J. Maag

Reedy Press
PO Box 5131
St. Louis, MO 63139
www.reedypress.com.

Library of Congress Control Number: 2020938253

ISBN: 9781681062938

Cover: *Images courtesy of Robert Pauly.*
Stations of the Volunteer Era: *Images courtesy of* History of the Volunteer Fire Department of St. Louis.
Badge, patch, and logos: Courtesy of the St. Louis Fire Department.
Stations of the Paid Fire Department Era, Other Fire Department Facilities, St. Louis Underwriters Salvage Corps, and Present Stations: *Images courtesy of Robert Pauley unless otherwise noted.*
Stations Today and The Survivors: *Images by Dennis J. Maag unless otherwise noted.*

Printed in the United States of America
20 21 22 23 24 5 4 3 2 1

TABLE OF CONTENTS

EBENEZER CHAPEL
OF THE
METHODIST EPISCOPAL
CHURCH

INTRODUCTION

The St. Louis Fire Department became a paid operation in 1857, only the second paid fire department in the United States. All of my life, I have been fascinated by the historical beauty of their stations, many of which I used to hang out in. Prior to 1857, there were twelve volunteer fire companies, and in the early years of the paid operation, St. Louis first used nine of their stations. As the years went on and the department grew, many new stations were built. Through the years, two fire stations were wood-frame construction, and there was even a temporary firehouse for protection at the 1904 World's Fair.

Over the years, more than sixty stations have served the St. Louis Fire Department, including four located at Lambert International Airport, one of which was also a temporary facility. The last new stations to be built included four during the 1960s and 1970s, all of which were one-story, ranch-style construction, a first for the St. Louis Fire Department.

The photos contained herein include all of the known fire stations along with information that is believed to be accurate at the time of this publication. The first section of the book details most of the former fire stations as well as some of the current stations as they appeared when originally constructed. These are all from my collection with many of the earlier images obtained from the collections of the late Neil Svetanics, former St. Louis fire chief; the late Harry Berne, former St. Louis Fire Department captain; the late Phil Nauman, former St. Louis Fire Department historian; and a few of mine as well. The second section of the book primarily contains images of the stations operated today but taken from the perspective of my reliable Kodak Brownie camera during the 1960s.

Many of the stations still in operation today retain their original historic characteristics but have received interior renovations to provide some of the comforts and needs for today's firefighters and their apparatus. It is my hope to share with you the history and beauty of the firehouses of the St. Louis Fire Department so you too may share in my enthusiasm.

This book took more time and effort than I expected, and I want to give a big thank-you to Dennis Maag who helped me along the way. I could not have completed this without his help. I would also like to thank Barbara Northcott of Reedy Press. Without her patience, direction, and keen eye for detail, the design and layout of this book would not have been possible.

—Robert Pauly, Curator
St. Louis Fire Department Museum

CANTON TEA C

THE START—STATIONS OF THE VOLUNTEER ERA

The St. Louis Volunteer Fire Department actually dates to around 1810 when the first apparatus was purchased. The North Side and South Side Fire Companies were formed in 1819, and from 1832 to 1856 ten companies operated from nine stations. In some cases, the volunteer companies dissolved, but in other cases they were incorporated into the paid fire department that formed in 1857.

Two additional fire companies formed after the paid fire department began—including the North St. Louis Volunteer Fire Department and Good Will Fire Company 11. These organizations were not affiliated with the St. Louis Volunteer Fire Department. They rented stations from disbanded fire companies and were not in existence very long.

CENTRAL FIRE COMPANY No. 1.

Located on the South Side of Chestnut Street, Between Third and Fourth Streets.

ENGINE HOUSE AND BURNING BUILDING,
Scene from an Actual Occurrence, February 6th, 1856.

CENTRAL FIRE COMPANY 1

South side of Chestnut Street, between Third and Fourth Streets

Central Fire Company 1 was in service from 1832 to 1859. This photo shows their second station, which was located on the south side of Chestnut Street between Third and Fourth Streets. Their motto was "Perseverance."

UNION FIRE COMPANY No. 2

Located on the West Side of Third Street, South of Washington Avenue.

NIGHT SCENE, VOLUNTEER TIMES OF 1855.
"Start Her Lively, Boys, the College Bell is Ringing!"

UNION FIRE COMPANY 2

Union Fire Company 2 operated from two stations during its existence from 1832 to 1855. This station was located on the west side of Third Street south of Washington. Their motto was "In Union There Is Strength." St. Louis Engine Company 2 continues to display the Union No. 2 logo on their apparatus that was original to the volunteers.

WASHINGTON FIRE COMPANY No. 3.

Located on the West Side of Third Street, between Elm Street and Clark Avenue

GETTING READY TO TAKE PART IN THE FIREMEN'S PARADE, MAY 1st, 1854.

WASHINGTON FIRE COMPANY 3

Washington Fire Company 3 operated from 1833 to 1857 from three different locations. This station was located on the west side of Third Street between Elm and Clark. Their motto was "Veni, Vidi, Vici" ("I came, I saw, I conquered"). This station also served as Station 3 for the paid fire department.

ST. LOUIS FIRE COMPANY No 4.

Located at the Southeast Corner of Third and Locust Streets.

WINTER SCENE IN VOLUNTEER TIMES, 1853.
"Away with Her, Boys! We Are in for a Cold Night's Work!"

ST. LOUIS FIRE COMPANY 4

St. Louis Fire Company 4 formed in 1839 and operated until 1859 from two different stations, including their second one shown here on the southwest corner of Third and Locust. Their motto was "On Hand."

MISSOURI FIRE COMPANY No. 5.

Located on the East Side of Third Street, South of Olive Street, adjoining the old St. Louis Theatre.

OLD ST. LOUIS THEATRE. MISSOURI FIRE COMPANY.

Testing the "Big Missouri," better known as "The Row Boat," June, 1852.

MISSOURI FIRE COMPANY 5

Missouri Fire Company 5 was only in existence for twenty years from (1839–1959), but they had four different facilities. Their last was this beautiful station located on the east side of Third Street south of Olive. Their motto was "Press On."

LIBERTY FIRE COMPANY No. 6.

Located at the Southwest Corner of Third Street and Franklin Avenue.

TRIAL OF THE NEW ENGINE, JUNE, 1852.

"Up and Down on Her, Boys!"

LIBERTY FIRE COMPANY 6

Liberty Fire Company 6 existed from 1841 to 1858, and they spared no expense on their only station, which was located on the southwest corner of Third and Franklin. In this image from 1852, members proudly display their new engine. Their motto, "We Conquer To Save," is evident here.

PHŒNIX FIRE COMPANY No. 7.

Located on the West Side of Broadway, just North of Park Avenue.

"Let Her Go With a Will, Boys! With a Will!"
VOLUNTEER DAYS OF 1854.

PHOENIX FIRE COMPANY 7

Phoenix Fire Company 7 existed from 1843 to 1858 and had two stations. This image shows their final location on the west side of Broadway just north of Park Avenue. This station was also used by Engine Company 6 and Engine Company 16 of the paid fire department. The volunteer motto was "Surgo Lucidos."

FRANKLIN FIRE COMPANY No. 8.

Located on the West Side of Eleventh Street, between Wash and Carr Streets.

CLEANING UP AFTER THE FIRE—VOLUNTEER DAYS OF 1856.

FRANKLIN FIRE COMPANY 8

During its existence from 1844 to 1858, Franklin Fire Company 8 occupied two stations. This image shows their last station, located on the west side of Eleventh between Wash and Carr. Their motto was "We Have The Enemy And They Are Ours." When the paid fire department took over, Engine Company 1 and later Engine Company 13 operated here.

MOUND FIRE COMPANY No. 9.

Located on the West Side of Broadway just South of Brooklyn Street.

BURNING OF THE PAVILION ON THE BIG MOUND, 1848.

MOUND FIRE COMPANY 9

Mound Fire Company 9 was home to this station, located on the west side of Broadway south of Brooklyn Street. During their volunteer days, their motto was "We Fly To Succo and Save." When the paid fire department took over, this station was used by Engine Company 4 and later Engine Company 9.

LACLEDE FIRE COMPANY No. 10

Located on the North Side of Market Street, just East of Fifteenth Street.

RECEIVING THE NEW ENGINE, OCTOBER, 1855.

LACLEDE FIRE COMPANY 10

Laclede Fire Company 10 operated for only ten years, and this was their station located on the north side of Market east of Fifteenth. Their motto was "Bon Accord." Engine Company 7 and later Engine Company 14 of the paid fire department also used this station.

STATIONS OF THE PAID FIRE DEPARTMENT

FIRE STATION 1

2411 McNair Avenue

Fire Station 1 opened in 1874 with Engine Company 1. In 1875, an addition was constructed to the south for a future hook and ladder company. In 1877, Hook and Ladder 1 moved in, and in 1896 District Chief 8 was organized here.

The station closed in 1971, with Engine Company 1 moving to Station 7 at 1304 South Eighteenth and Hook and Ladder 1 moving to Station 11 at 2224 South Seventh Street. The building at 2411 McNair Avenue is still standing today and is privately owned.

FIRE STATION 2

On Washington Avenue between Seventh and Eighth Streets

Fire Station 2 opened in 1857 and was assigned Engine Company 2. In 1859, Engine 2 was relocated to the quarters of the former Franklin Volunteer Fire Company, located on the south side of Franklin Avenue between Twenty-Second and Twenty-Third Streets. At that time, Engine Company 5 was assigned here. They operated until 1867 when they were taken out of service. The station was closed and torn down a short time later.

FIRE STATION 2

On the south side of Franklin Avenue between Twenty-Second and Twenty-Third Streets

This station was originally built and occupied by the Franklin Volunteer Fire Company. In 1859, Engine Company 2 was assigned here and operated until 1871 when they were assigned to a new station at 129 West Krause. This station was closed and razed. This photo shows the company with paid personnel.

FIRE STATION 2

508 North Third Street

This station opened in 1885 and was home to Engine Company 23, Hook and Ladder 6, and Chemical Company 3. In 1890, Water Tower 1 was organized and assigned to the station, with Chemical Company 3 being removed from service during in 1891. In 1896, Water Tower 1 was relocated to another station. Assignments remained the same until 1903 when Engine 23 moved to a new station located at 129 Krause. Engine Company 2 was relocated here from their previous location in Carondelet as the administration felt that Engine 2 should be a downtown company. In 1941, this station was closed, with Engine Company 2 being relocated to Station 24 at 314 South Twelfth Street and Hook and Ladder 6 relocated to Station 6 at 12 North Ninth Street.

It is believed that the first fire department repair shop was located in the basement of the building and operated here until 1902 when it moved to a new repair shop at 2000 Washington Avenue. Note the Union No. 2 signage at the top of the building as well as above the right apparatus bay.

Interior view of the station shows the horse stalls in the back of the apparatus floor during the horse-drawn era. A closer look on the left side of the photo reveals the rear of the aerial ladder.

Photo courtesy of the Missouri Historical Society

FIRE STATION 3

Carondelet Avenue and Capital Street (later known as 3648 South Broadway and Salena)

This station opened in 1874 for Engine Company 3 and was remodeled and rebuilt from a farmer's market located on the site. In 1875, an addition was built on the south side of the station for Fuel Wagon 4. That same year, a handball court was constructed for the firemen adjacent to the new addition. Engine Company 3 operated here until 1918 when the building, deteriorated beyond repair, was torn down and a new station was built on the same site. During construction, Engine Company 3 operated from temporary quarters at 3635 South Broadway in a building formerly used as a garage.

Note the firefighter in front of the station with a dalmatian. Dalmatians were known for their stamina, endurance, and ability to calm the horses. These traits made them an ideal addition to fire stations during this time.

FIRE STATION 3

3648 South Broadway

This newly constructed station opened in 1919 on the same parcel of land as the former Station 3. It was home to Engine Company 3 and Gasoline Supply Truck 4 when it was completed. The station closed in 1969, and Engine Company 3 was taken out of service. This building is still owned by the city of St. Louis and its exterior has been wonderfully preserved. It cannot be sold as the land would have to be returned to the heirs of the original owners.

When viewing the hose tower on the right rear of the station, note how the brickwork for the chimney is nicely concealed in it. Note also the black bunting below the second-floor windows above the bay door, presumably for a line-of-duty firefighter death.

FIRE STATION 4

2233 Cole Street

This station opened in 1871 for General Lyon Engine Company 4 who had been operating from the station formerly operated by volunteer Mound Fire Company 9. General Nathanial Lyon was a commander of the Union arsenal in St. Louis and was the first Union general to be killed in the Civil War. Engine 4 operated as the lone company until 1931 when Water Tower 1 was assigned here. In 1933, Engine Company 4 was removed from service, Water Tower 1 was assigned to another location, and the station closed. It was later torn down.

FIRE STATION 5

216 North Seventh Street

This station was originally constructed and operated by the volunteers of Missouri Fire Company 5. The paid fire department assigned Engine Company 5 here in 1858, but they only operated here until 1859. They were then relocated to Fire Station 2 on Washington Avenue between Seventh and Eighth Streets and operated there until 1867 when they were taken out of service. That same year, St. Louis organized Hook and Ladder 1, which was assigned to this station alone until 1869 when Engine Company 5 was reactivated. In 1872, Hook and Ladder 1 was relocated to Station 3 at 415 South Fifth. At that time, Hook and Ladder Company 2 was organized and operated alongside Engine Company 5 until 1874 when both companies were reassigned to a new station at 2400 North Twenty-Second Street. Engine Company 6 was then assigned here as was newly organized Hook and Ladder 3 with these companies operating until 1902 when they were reassigned. Over the years, this station also served as fire department headquarters and was home to Fuel Wagon 1. From 1878–1898, ten brave firefighters who were assigned to this station lost their lives in the line of duty. The station was permanently closed in 1902 and later razed.

FIRE STATION 5

2400 North Twenty-Second Street

This building was constructed and opened in 1874 to house Engine Company 5 and Hook and Ladder 2. Adjacent to this station was the fire department warehouse and horse hospital. In 1953, a new station was constructed a short distance away at 2123 North Market, and both companies were relocated there. Following their departure, Fire Alarm used the building for storage purposes for several years until the station was closed and later torn down.

FIRE STATION 6

12 North Ninth Street

Station 6 opened in 1902 and was the new home to Engine Company 6 and Hook and Ladder 3. Both units operated here until 1933 when Hook and Ladder 3 was relocated. When the station was closed for remodeling in 1939, Engine Company 6 was temporarily relocated to Station 24 at 314 South Twelfth Street. It reopened in 1941, and Engine Company 6 returned. Other companies assigned here included Hook and Ladder 6 from 1941 to 1942, Gas Truck 1 and Foam Truck 1 from 1942 to 1943, and the Canteen Truck from 1943 to 1944. Rescue Squad 1 also ran from Station 6 from 1943 until it closed in 1965. At that time, Engine Company 6 was taken out of service and Rescue Squad 1 was relocated to Fire Station 2 at 314 South Twelfth Street. Fire Station 6 was eventually torn down. Note the St. Louis Fire Department lettering at the top of the building and the ornate design between the second- and third-floor windows.

Photo of Leon Sutton in the Joker Room at Fire Station 6 in the 1960s.

Interior view of the apparatus floor of Fire Station 6 taken in the 1940s. On the left is Rescue Squad 1's 1947 International, on the right is Pumper 6's 1926 Ahrens-Fox 1300-GPM pumper, and in the rear is a 1935 Studebaker that was the fire department canteen. Note the ornate ceiling covering with the various flags on display.

FIRE STATION 7

1304 South Eighteenth Street

Fire Station 7 opened in 1873, and Engine Company 7 operated here until the station was destroyed by a tornado in 1896. The photo below shows the complete destruction of Fire Station 7 after the tornado, which killed two horses and badly damaged the apparatus. Fortunately no fireman were injured. A new station was constructed on the same lot, opening in 1897.

The 1896 tornado was one of the deadliest in US history, killing over 200 people and causing millions in damage.

FIRE STATION 7

1304 South Eighteenth Street

This Station opened in 1897 on the same lot as the original Station 7, which was destroyed by a tornado in 1896. In addition to Engine Company 7, Hook and Ladder 14 was assigned here from 1905 to 1942. In 1942, Hose Wagon 5 was organized an operated alongside Engine 7. From 1963 to 1965, Engine Company 33 was located here so Engine 21 and Hook and Ladder 5 could use Station 33 while a new building was being constructed for them. In 1971, Engine Company 7 was relocated to a newly constructed station at 2600 LaSalle Street. At that time, Engine Company 1 was relocated here and operated until 1975 when they moved to their new station at 2910 South Jefferson.

This station closed in 1975 but remains standing and is privately owned.

Hook and Ladder 14

FIRE STATION 8

1501 Salisbury Street

Station 8 opened in 1865 for Engine Company 8. In 1927, the station was badly damaged by a tornado and torn down.

Note the beautiful frontispiece raised above the roof line and featuring Engine No. 8. Looking to the left of the station, you can see the iron fence and entrance to Hyde Park.

A new station was built on the same site during which time Engine Company 8 relocated to Station 20. Completed in 1928, Engine Company 8 continues to operate from the station today.

1921 American LaFrance pumper assigned to Station 8

FIRE STATION 9

On North Broadway between Mound and Brooklyn

Fire Station 9 was originally built during the volunteer era and operated by Mound Fire Company 9. When the St. Louis Fire Department began their paid operation in 1857, Engine Company 4 was assigned here and remained until 1871 when they were relocated to the station at 2233 Cole Street. At that time, Engine Company 9 was assigned here and operated until 1885 when they moved into a new station at 1545 North Eighth Street. This station closed at that time and was later torn down.

This is the only known photo of the station and company.

FIRE STATION 9

1545 North Eighth Street

Station 9 opened in 1885 with Engine Company 9 and newly organized Hook and Ladder 7, as evidenced by the lettering above the bay door. Water Tower 2 was also assigned to this station from 1942 to 1954. In 1957, Engine Company 9 and Hook and Ladder 7 moved to a new station at 814 La Beaume Street, resulting in this beautiful station being closed and torn down.

FIRE STATION 10

20 South Jefferson Avenue

Fire Station 10 opened in 1867 for Engine Company 10. This station was closed in 1914 and torn down to make way for a new Fire Station 10 on the same site. Barely visible in the photos are the firefighters in their dress uniforms.

Interior view of the apparatus floor at the original Fire Station 10, built in 1867. Note the crew posed around the watch desk and horses in the stalls behind the apparatus.

FIRE STATION 10

20 South Jefferson Avenue

This photo shows the second station to be constructed at 20 South Jefferson for Engine Company 10. This station opened in 1914 and was operated until 1942 when Engine Company 10 was relocated to the station at 4161 Kennerly. This building was later torn down.

Interior view of the apparatus bay of Station 10 shortly after it opened in 1914. The apparatus for Engine 10 is a 1913 Robinson 900-GPM pumper.

FIRE STATION 11

2400 South Fourth Street

This station opened in 1867 for the newly organized Engine Company 9. In 1871, Engine Company 9 was relocated to a different station and Engine Company 11 was organized and assigned to this station. They used this building until 1908 when a new fire station was constructed at the same location. This is the only known photo of this station.

FIRE STATION 11

2400 South Fourth Street

This station opened in 1908 on the same site as the original station and was home to Engine Company 11 as well as Foam Truck 1 from 1936 to 1942. In 1939, Engine Company 45 was assigned here but only served until 1942 when they were taken out of service. Hose Wagon 3 was assigned here from 1942 to 1949, and in 1961 Engine Company 16 was assigned here. In 1963, Engine Companies 11 and 16 moved to a new station at 2224 South Seventh. The station that opened in 1908 was closed in 1963 and later torn down. Note the unique design in the brickwork.

FIRE STATION 12 & 18

818 North Seventh Street

This station opened in 1872 and was assigned Engine Company 12. Fire Department Headquarters also relocated here from their former location at 216 North Seventh Street. In 1875, Engine Company 18 was organized and operated from this station as well. Fire Department Headquarters moved to Room 104 of the new city hall at 1200 Market in 1901. In 1928, Gasoline Supply Truck 6 was organized and stationed here. In 1933, Engine Company 12 was taken out of service and the following year Gasoline Supply Truck 6 was also removed from service. In 1939, Station 12–18 was closed, with Engine Company 18 being moved to Station 2 at 508 North Third Street. This station was torn down several years later. Note the large canvas awnings over the windows and entry door.

FIRE STATION 13

1015 North Eleventh Street

This station was originally built and operated by Franklin Fire Company 8 during the volunteer era. When the paid operation began in 1857, this station was used by Engine Company 1, which operated here until 1874 when they moved to their new station at 2411 McNair Avenue. At that time, newly organized Engine Company 13 was assigned to this station and operated here until 1933 when they were taken out of service and the station closed. The building at 1015 North Eleventh was torn down the following year. Note the designs in the concrete at the corners and above the apparatus bay door.

FIRE STATION 14

1425 Market Street

This station was originally built and operated by Laclede Fire Company 10 during the volunteer era. When the paid operation began, Engine Company 7 was assigned here in 1858. They operated at this station until 1873 when they moved into their new station at 1304 South Eighteenth Street. Upon their departure, newly organized Engine Company 14 was assigned here and operated until 1929 when they moved to a new station located at 314 South Twelfth Street with Engine Company 24. The station closed in 1929 and was torn down some time later.

Note the interesting construction on the front of the building and unique graphics in the concrete.

Photo courtesy of the Missouri Historical Society

FIRE STATION 14 & 24

314 South Twelfth Street

Opened in 1929, Engine Companies 14 and 24 were initially assigned here. In 1933, Engine Company 14 was taken out of service and Water Tower 1 was assigned here instead. Other companies assigned here over the years included Rescue Squad 1 in 1934, Foam Truck 2 in 1936, and Engine Company 2 in 1941. In 1942, Engine 24 relocated to Station 53 at 5345 Natural Bridge Avenue, and Water Tower 1 was permanently removed from service. Rescue Squad 1 and Foam Truck 2 also were reassigned to other stations.

Today, this station is occupied by Engine Company 2, Hook and Ladder 2, Chemical Unit 1, Battalion Chief 2, and Medic 2. In fitting tribute to this old station, St. Louis's beautifully restored 1927 Ahrens-Fox is stored here as well.

FIRE STATION 15 AND 39

415 South Broadway

This station opened in 1864 for Engine Company 3 and was built after their former station at 211 South Third was destroyed by fire. In 1872, an addition was constructed on the south side of the building, and when it was completed, Hook and Ladder 1 was assigned to the new building. In 1874, Engine Company 3 moved to a new fire station at Carondelet and Capital. Upon their departure, Engine Company 15 was organized and assigned here along with Chemical Company 1. In 1877, Hook and Ladder 1 was reassigned to their new station at 2411 McNair Avenue, and Hook and Ladder Company 4 was organized and assigned here. In 1900, Chemical Company 1 was removed from service and replaced by newly organized Engine Company 39. This station closed in 1929, and a new station was built on the same site for Engine Companies 15 and 39, Hook and Ladder 4, and Hose Wagon 1.

Fuel Wagon 2 operated here from 1868 to 1885.

FIRE STATION 15 AND 39

415 South Broadway

This station opened in 1929 on the same site as the original station that opened in 1864. When reopened, Engine Companies 15 and 39, Hook and Ladder 4, and Hose Wagon 1 operated here. Hose Wagon 1 moved to Station 40–41 in 1942, and in 1960 Engine Company 39 was permanently taken out of service. Hook and Ladder 4 was taken out of service in 1963 and replaced by the St. Louis Fire Department's first snorkel. Snorkel Company 1 was assigned a 1963 FWD chassis with Towers bodywork and a Pitman 85-foot boom. In 1969, Engine Company 15 was taken out of service, and the snorkel was reassigned to Station 2 at 314 South Tucker Boulevard. The station at 415 South Broadway was closed, torn down, and became a parking area for the new Busch Stadium. The station would be located in right field of the current Busch Stadium. Note the two L-Model Mack pumpers and snorkel in the station.

FIRE STATION 16

1337 South Broadway

This station was originally built and operated by Phoenix Fire Company 7 during the volunteer years. After the paid operation began, Engine Company 6 was assigned here in 1858. They operated here until 1874 when Engine Company 6 moved into a different station at 216 North Seventh Street. Upon their departure, newly organized Engine Company 16 was assigned here and occupied this station until 1961 when they moved to a new station along with Engine Company 11 at 2224 South Seventh Street. The station at 1337 South Broadway closed in 1961 after 115 years of service to St. Louis and was torn down some time later.

FIRE STATION 17

3220 Easton Avenue

Fire Station 17 opened in 1874 for Engine Company 17. A new station was constructed adjacent to this station and opened in 1925. When Engine Company 17 moved into the new station, the original station that faced Easton Avenue was torn down.

FIRE STATION 18

223 South Newstead Avenue

Fire Station 18 opened in 1913 for Engine Company 50 and Hook and Ladder Company 19. In 1942, Engine Company 50 was permanently removed from service, and Engine Company 18 was assigned to this station as a replacement. Hook and Ladder 19 was permanently removed from service in 1974, and Rescue Squad 1 was temporarily assigned here.

In 1975, Engine Company 18 was reassigned to 3324 Park Avenue, and Rescue Squad 1 was reassigned to Station 1 on South Jefferson. This station closed and was later torn down.

This photograph shows the station after modifications were made to the front of the building to accommodate a larger apparatus bay door. The ornate brickwork above the roof line has also been removed.

FIRE STATION 19

1120 St. Louis Avenue

Fire Station 19 opened in 1878 for Engine Company 19, and for a number of years District Chief 5 was also assigned here. In 1933, Engine Company 19 was taken out of service, and the station was closed and torn down.

In 1937, St. Louis Municipal Bath House No. 6 was built on the site of former Fire Station 19. It was the last bathhouse built in the city of St. Louis and remained open until 1965. The structure still stands today. Note the interesting woodwork on the upper portions of the apparatus bay doors.

FIRE STATION 20

4551 North Broadway

Fire Station 20 opened in 1880 and was assigned Engine Company 20. In 1897, construction was completed on the south side of the structure that doubled the size of the station and permitted housing for newly established Hook and Ladder Company 12. Additional companies assigned here included Fuel Wagon 11, Gas Truck 3, and Hose Wagon 7, which was established at the station in 1942. In 1960, this station was closed, and Engine Company 20, Hook and Ladder 12, and Hose Wagon 7 all moved into a new one-story fire station located at 5600 Prescott Avenue. This building was torn down a short time later. Note the man doors in each of the bay doors to permit the passage of personnel without opening the bay door.

FIRE STATION 21

3517 Market Street

Fire Station 21 opened in 1883 for the newly formed companies of Engine 21 and Hook and Ladder 5. Fuel Supply Truck 1 was also located here for a number of years. In 1928, the companies moved to a new station at 3407 West Market. This station closed and was later torn down.

When the station opened in 1883, this section of Market was known as Manchester Road.

FIRE STATION 21

3407 Market Street

This station opened in 1928, not far from the original Fire Station 21. At the time, Engine Company 21 and Hook and Ladder Company 5 were assigned here as was District Chief 7. Foam Truck 2 was stationed here from 1943 to 1955. The fire department's 1957-1958 annual report indicates that this "perfectly good structure which would otherwise be good for many years of service" would soon be razed for the Mill Creek Redevelopment Project, designed to redevelop the decaying neighborhood of tenements and slums. In 1965, Engine Company 21, Hook and Ladder Company 5, and District Chief 7 all relocated to a new station at 200 South Vandeventer.

Note the clay tile roof and exterior window coverings, more typical of a residence than a fire station.

FIRE STATION 22

116 Plum Street

Fire Station 22 opened in 1885 at 116 South Plum Street. It featured a three-story tower and was home to Engine Company 22 and Fuel Wagon 2. The station closed in 1914 when Engine Company 22 moved to a new station at 831 South Sixth Street. It was reported that the station was closed and relocated due to the continued vibration caused by the frequent train traffic nearby.

FIRE STATION 22

831 South Sixth Street

This station opened in 1914 and was the second station for Engine Company 22. It also provided quarters for Gas Truck 8 until 1933 when they were taken out of service. The station was located next to the Municipal Bridge, also known as the Free Bridge, which later became a toll bridge. It featured a 55-foot clock tower and housed a library on the second floor. The clock was for bridge users coming from Illinois to know what time it was when they were arriving in St. Louis. In 1942, the bridge was renamed the McArthur Bridge in honor of General Douglas McArthur. That same year, Engine Company 22 relocated to the station at 6810 Clayton Avenue, which was formerly Station 52, and this station closed. The McArthur Bridge remains an important span across the Mississippi River for both Illinois and Missouri residents.

FIRE STATION 23

129 West Krause Street

This station opened in 1871 for Engine Company 2, and in 1877 Fuel Wagon 5 moved in. In 1882, an addition was constructed that led to Chemical and Ladder Company 2 being assigned here in 1883. They operated until 1895 when they were replaced by the newly organized Hook and Ladder Company 11. In 1903, Engine Company 2 was assigned to a new station at 508 North Third Street, and Engine Company 23 was assigned here. Engine Company 23 and Hook and Ladder 11 operated here until 1921 when they moved to a new station at 6500 Michigan Avenue. This station was closed and torn down. Note the dirt street in front of the station.

FIRE STATION 23

6500 Michigan Avenue

Fire Station 23 opened in 1921 for Engine Company 23, Hook and Ladder 11, Fuel Wagon 5, and District Chief 10. Over the years, the Fuel Wagon and District Chief were moved to other stations, and Hook and Ladder 11 was removed from service in 1986. Medic 1 moved to this station in 1999 and was renumbered Medic 23.

Today, Engine Company 23 and Medic 23 protect the residents and businesses in the Carondelet neighborhood on the city's south side. This station has the distinction of being the only one in St. Louis to have roman numerals for the company number above the apparatus door.

FIRE STATION 24

1214 Spruce Street

This station opened in 1884 for Engine Company 24 and was located near the red light district. On October 15, 1899, there was a murder not far from Station 24 at 212 Targee Street that later became the story line for the famous song "Frankie and Johnny."

In 1921, the St. Louis Fire Department hired their first black firefighters, and they had the distinction of being assigned to Station 24. They remained together as a fire company and were later transferred to Station 28.

This station closed in 1929 and was torn down. Note the area in the brickwork at the top of the building with the year of construction—1884.

Firefighter Walter Rebman on Joker Watch at Station 25. Note the Gamewell System on the shelf in the background.

FIRE STATION 25

1600 North Sixteenth Street

Station 25 opened in 1885 and was initially assigned Engine Company 25. District Chief 4 was later stationed here, and Hose Wagon 4 was established in 1942.

Station 25 holds the distinction of being the last station with a horse-drawn company assigned to it, their last run occurring on March 25, 1927. The horses were Tom & Jerry and Monk & Strawberry.

In 1953, Engine Company 25 and Hose Wagon 4 moved to the Station at 2123 North Market, as the station at 1600 North Sixteenth was closed and torn down. Note the large American flag flying above the bay door.

FIRE STATION 26

2100 North Second Street

Located just two blocks west of the banks of the Mississippi River, Station 26 opened in 1887. Engine Company 26 was assigned here and operated until 1942 when they moved to the station at 4520 Margaretta that had formerly been home to Engine Company 54.

The station at 2100 North Second Street was closed and has been operated by a variety of businesses over the years, the last being American Timber Salvage. The building was for sale in 2018 with an asking price of $250,000.

FIRE STATION 26

2100 North Second Street

This photo was taken by Robert Pauly in 1964 when the building was owned by the Eberius Elevator Company. Note some of the changes to the building including the removal of the dormer from the front of the roof as well as one of the chimneys on the south side of the building.

FIRE STATION 27

4571 Easton Avenue

This station located at 4571 Easton Avenue opened in 1885 and was originally built for Chemical Company 4. But shortly after the station opened, the company moved to a station at 3934 Enright Avenue and were replaced by Chemical Company 5. They only operated until 1888 when Engine Company 27 was established, replacing Chemical Company 5. The 27s operated here until 1932 when they moved to the station located at 4810 Enright. The station was closed in 1932.

Below is the running card for the station.

2713 M.L. KING & CORA				
ENGINE	H&L	OFF	SQ	
28–10–26	15	5	2	4,600
17–24–17	9	1		W
30–29–5	3			1,500
12–20–8	SNT			N
6–7–9				

On July 17, 1985, former Fire Station 27 at 4571 Dr. Martin Luther King Drive (formerly Easton Avenue) was being torn down when the building collapsed trapping several workers from the demolition crew in the rubble.

The St. Louis Fire Department struck two alarms and two special calls for additional equipment to aid in the rescue effort. Companies responding were:

	ENGINE	H&L	OFF	SQ
First Alarm	28–10–26	15	5	2
Second Alarm	17–24–17	9	1	
Special Call 1		3, SN 5		1
Special Call 2		2, 7, 14–05		

Firefighters worked for more than three hours rescuing and treating five workers. Despite their efforts, a sixth worker who was trapped died from his injuries.

FIRE STATION 28

3934 Enright Avenue (formerly Morgan Avenue)

This station at 3934 Morgan Avenue (later known as Enright Avenue) originally opened in 1885, operating with Chemical Company 4. In 1888, newly established Engine Company 28 replaced Chemical Company 4 and operated until 1893 when Hook and Ladder 9 was established. In 1929, the station became integrated when black firefighters transferred in from Station 24.

In 1952, an accident occurred at Vandeventer and Easton when Hook and Ladder 9 and Engine Company 17 collided, killing three firefighters. William Grady of Hook and Ladder Company 9 was one of those killed. He was the first black firefighter killed in the line of duty.

In 1960, Engine Company 28 moved to Station 43, and Hook and Ladder 9 moved to Station 10 (temporarily operating a 65-foot aerial due to station limitations) while Station 28 was torn down and a new station was built on the same site.

FIRE STATION 28

3934 Enright Avenue (formerly known as Morgan Avenue)

This station opened in 1961 on the site of the original Fire Station 28. Engine Company 28 and Hook and Ladder 9 moved back into the station from their temporary reassignments. The station cost $115,385 to build but was only occupied until 1965 when Engine Company 28 moved to a different station and Hook and Ladder 9 was taken out of service.

In the modern history of the St. Louis Fire Department, it marks the shortest time a station was occupied. The building still exists and has been nicely renovated as a private home.

Fire Station 28 was only open for four years.

FIRE STATION 29

1219 South Vandeventer (formerly Old Manchester Avenue)

This station opened in 1888 for Engine Company 29, which operated here until 1965 when they moved to a new station at 200 South Vandeventer. Station 29 was closed, but the building remains and is the home of a private business. Note the markings for the company on the front of the building, the only St. Louis fire station lettered as such.

FIRE STATION 30

5524 Vernon Avenue

Fire Station 30 opened in 1892, and Engine Company 30 operated here until 1957 when they moved to a brand-new station at 541 DeBaliviere Avenue. The original Station 30 was closed and torn down. Note the two-piece steamer and hose company assigned to Engine Company 30 at the time of this photo.

FIRE STATION 31

3945 Kossuth Avenue

This station opened in 1892 and was assigned Engine Company 31. It was located in North St. Louis just across the street from what later became known as Fairground Park. In 1907, District Chief 11 was established and assigned to Station 31. This station was closed in 1953, and Engine Company 31 was relocated to a brand-new station at 4408 Donovan Avenue in South St. Louis. The station at 3945 Kossuth Avenue was torn down, and today the lot is home to a private residence.

FIRE STATION 32

2000 Washington Avenue

Fire Station 32 opened in 1892 and was assigned Engine Company 32, Hook and Ladder 8, Fuel Wagon 8, and Chemical Company 4, which was reactivated after previously being removed from service. The large two-story/two-bay structure was situated on Washington Avenue facing north with the company numbers embossed on the front of the building. In 1896, a new style of fire apparatus, Water Tower 2, was placed into service, and Chemical Company 4 was permanently placed out of service. In 1902, Fuel Wagon 7 transferred into this station, working alongside Fuel Wagon 8. It is believed to be the only time that two fuel wagons were assigned together at the same station.

In 1919, Engine Company 32 and Hook and Ladder 8 moved into a new station that was built at 503 North Twentieth Street, adjacent to the south side of the existing station on Washington Avenue. At this time, former Fire Station 32 on Washington Avenue became the fire department repair shop.

The repair shop portion of this building was razed, but the old fire station remains standing today and is home to the Brick River Cider Company.

FIRE STATION 32

503 North Twentieth Street

This station opened in 1919 with the companies only having to relocate around the corner from their previous station on Washington Avenue as the new building is immediately adjacent to the rear of the former station. Engine Company 32 and Hook and Ladder 8 operated at this location until 1971 when they moved to Station 7 on LaSalle Street.

The building at 503 North Twentieth Street is still standing and is a privately owned residence.

Fire Station 32 cost $26,561.07 to construct.

FIRE STATION 33

3324 Park Avenue

Station 33 opened on Park Avenue in 1895 for Engine Company 33. Hose Wagon 8 was organized in 1942 and operated here until 1949. In 1963, Engine Company 33 was temporarily relocated to Fire Station 7, which made space for Engine Company 21 and Hook and Ladder 5 to move into Station 33 while their new station was being built. In 1965, these two companies moved into their new station at 200 South Vandeventer along with Engine Company 29. At that point, Engine Company 33 moved back into Station 33 and operated here until 1975. At that time, they were relocated to the station at 8300 North Broadway where they continue to operate today. Beautiful Station 33 was officially closed on April 2, 1975, after nearly eighty years of service to the city of St. Louis. It was torn down in 1992.

FIRE STATION 35

5450 Arsenal Street

Fire Station 35 opened in August 1895. Interestingly, it opened before Fire Station 34. The new building was home for Engine Company 35 and Hook and Ladder 10. This photo shows the station as it looked when it was newly built. Note the beautiful arched opening, wooden doors, and company numbers set in the brick. This building was remodeled in 1959–1960 and is presently home to Truck 35, Medic 35, and Battalion Chief 803.

FIRE STATION 36

1719 North Union Boulevard

This station opened in 1911 on the same parcel of land as the original Station 36 (for which there is no known photo). On July 27, 1910, the first motorized apparatus, a 1910 Webb 700-GPM pumper, was placed into service. Initially it was rotated to companies throughout the city for training. It was later assigned to Engine 36 as seen in this photo. Engine Company 36 operated here until August 8, 1942, when they moved to former Station 56 at 5000 South Kingshighway. The station at 1719 North Union Boulevard is still standing today and is privately owned.

FIRE STATION 37

8300 North Broadway

This station located in the Baden area of North St. Louis opened in 1897 for Engine Company 37. This was one of only two wood frame fire stations operated by the St. Louis Fire Department, and it was only in service until 1909. It was torn down, and a new station was built nearby.

FIRE STATION 37

8300 North Broadway

This station opened in 1909, very close to the location of the original Fire Station 37. Engine Company 37 operated as the lone company until 1932 when Hook and Ladder Company 3 was reassigned here. In 1976, Engine Company 37 and Hook and Ladder 3 were taken permanently out of service. At that time, Engine Company 33 was reassigned here. In 1999, Medic 33 was assigned here and continues to work today alongside Engine 33. Note the uniquely designed brickwork above the roof line.

FIRE STATION 38

3500 South Grand Avenue

This station opened on February 20, 1899, for Engine Company 38 and operated alone until 1905 when Hook and Ladder Company 16 was organized and assigned here. Additional companies assigned here over the years included Inhalator Company 2 from 1933 to 1942 and Gas Truck 4 in 1935. In 1942, Hook and Ladder 16 moved to 4425 South Compton Avenue, and their vacancy was filled by the newly organized Hose Wagon 6. In 1955, Gas Truck 2 was also assigned here. Hose Wagon 6 was taken out of service in 1971, and in 1976 Engine Company 38 was permanently taken out of service and replaced by Engine Company 32. They operated with Hook and Ladder 14 until 1986 when the Total Quint Concept was implemented, and the hook and ladder was removed from service. Engine 32 continues to operate at this station today along with Medic 32.

Note the crew peering from the windows of the apparatus bay doors (firefighter antics haven't changed over the years!). Note also the concrete work on either side of the bay doors. It is not known if these were originally windows that have been filled or perhaps used to display posters.

FIRE STATION 40 & 41

707 North Eleventh Street

This station opened on March 1, 1904, with Engine Companies 40 and 41 as well as Hook and Ladder Company 13. Over the years, a number of other companies were assigned to this station including Hose Wagon 2 (1928–1942), Inhalator Company 1 (1933–1942), Engine Company 18 (1941–1942), and Hose Wagon 1 was the last assigned in 1942. In 1956, Engine Companies 40 and 41, Hook and Ladder 13, and Hose Wagon 1 all moved to a new station at 921 Delmar Boulevard, about two blocks east. Station 40 and 41 was closed at that time, but the building is still standing today and is privately owned and operated as a business. Note the station decorated for Centennial Day in this view.

FIRE STATION 40 & 41

921 Delmar Boulevard

This station opened on October 24, 1956, with Engine Companies 40 and 41, Hook and Ladder 13, and Hose Wagon 1 moving here from the former station at 707 North Eleventh. Battalion Chief 1 joined them in this new station, which boasted larger apparatus bays for the larger modern apparatus as compared to their old station. In 1973, Hose Wagon 1 was taken out of service. And in 1975, as the St. Louis Fire Department reduced companies, Engine Company 40 became Engine Company 15 and Engine Company 41 became Engine Company 25. They operated here until June 11, 1978, when this station was closed to make way for the construction of the Cervantes Convention Center. The companies moved to other stations, Engine 15 to Station 2 and Engine 25 to Station 9, where they operated until 1981 when both companies were permanently removed from service. This building was razed in 1978. This was one of several similar stations built during this era for multiple fire companies.

FIRE STATION 42

5747 Manchester Avenue

This station opened on January 22, 1905, on Manchester Avenue, which is also Missouri Highway 100. Engine Company 42 relocated from their World's Fair fire station and operated until April 2, 1975, when fire department reorganization saw it taken out of service and replaced by Engine Company 6. Interestingly, several hook and ladder companies were briefly assigned to this station including Hook and Ladder 18 from 1957 to 1958 and Hook and Ladder 10 from 1959 to 1960 and again from 1986 to 1987. This station continues to be operated today by Engine Company 6. Note the ornate decorations above the second-floor windows and the tall tilt-in windows on the front of the building on either side of the apparatus bay doors.

FIRE STATION 43

732 North Kingshighway

Fire Station 43 opened on May 1, 1905, with Engine Company 43, Hook and Ladder 15, and Fuel Wagon 10. These companies operated here for only twenty-seven years when they moved to a new, much larger station at 4810 Enright Avenue on June 18, 1932. This station was closed and later torn down.

FIRE STATION 43

4810 Enright Avenue

Station 43 opened on June 18, 1932, just a couple of blocks east of their original station at 732 North Kingshighway. When the station opened, Engine Company 43 and Hook and Ladder 15 moved here. Note the beautiful building with dormers above each of the bay doors and the small addition on the right (west) side of the building that served as the Joker Room. For a ten-year period from 1932 to 1942, Engine Company 27 was also assigned to this station.

Other companies assigned to this station over the years included:

- Inhalator Company 3 (1933–1942)
- Rescue Squad 1 (1966–1974)
- Hose Wagon 12 (1949–1966)
- Hose Wagon 10 (1942–1946)

On April 2, 1975, as part of the fire department restructuring, Engine Company 43 was permanently taken out of service and Engine Company 28 was assigned to this station. They continue to operate from this station today along with Hook and Ladder 5 (renumbered in 2009), the HazMat Task Force, and Battalion Chief 5.

FIRE STATION 44

4425 South Compton Avenue

This station opened in 1906 with Engine Company 44. They operated here until 1942 when they were taken out of service and replaced by Engine Company 4. Today Truck 4 operates from this station along with Battalion Chief 4. Note the proud officer posing in front of the station.

FIRE STATION 45

914 Allen Avenue

This station opened on March 1, 1906, only a few blocks from the famous Soulard Market. Engine Company 45 was assigned here and operated until June 16, 1939, when they were relocated to Fire Station 11 at 2400 South Fourth Street. Engine 45 was taken out of service in 1942 while at Station 11. The station was closed at that time, but the building is still standing today and is beautifully preserved as a private residence.

FIRE STATION 46

4161 Kennerly Avenue

This station opened in February 1908 and was home to Engine Company 46. In 1942, Engine Company 46 was taken out of service and replaced by Engine Company 10. Today, Truck 10 and Medic 10 continue to operate from this location.

FIRE STATION 47

5214 West Florissant Avenue

This station opened in December 1909 for Engine Company 47.

They operated here until 1942 when they were taken out of service and replaced by Engine Company 12. They operated until 2009 when Hook and Ladder 6 was reactivated, rendering Engine 12 out of service. They continue to serve as the only company from this station today.

Note the ornate brickwork above the roofline similar to Fire Station 37, which was built the same year. Also note the firefighters on the parapet, presumably after raising the American flag.

FIRE STATION 48

1400 Shawmut Place

Fire Station 48 opened in 1909 and at that time was home to newly organized Engine Company 48 and Hook and Ladder 17. During a restructuring of the department in 1942, Engine Company 48 was taken out of service and Engine Company 13 was reorganized and took their place at this station. In 1946, Hose Wagon 10 was assigned here and operated until 1971. In another department restructuring that took place in 1976, Hook and Ladder 17 was permanently removed from service and Hook and Ladder 3 was reorganized. They operated until 1987 when St. Louis implemented the Total Quint Concept and Hook and Ladder 3 was once again taken out of service. This beautiful station's interior was renovated in the first decade of the twenty-first century, and it's now home to Truck 13 and Medic 13.

FIRE STATION 49

3523 Magnolia Avenue

This beautiful station opened in November 1909 for Engine Company 49. They operated here until a reorganization occurred in 1942 when Engine Company 49 was taken out of service and replaced by Engine Company 14. Hook and Ladder 14 was assigned here the same year and operated for thirty-four years, including a brief period utilizing their Aerialscope. In 1976 when they moved to Station 32. Engine 14 and Medic 14 continue to operate today in this station that maintains much of its original beauty. Note the large tilt-out windows above the bay door and ornate concrete work above the roofline.

FIRE STATION 50

223 South Newstead Avenue

This station opened on March 13, 1913, with Engine Company 50 and Hook and Ladder Company 19 assigned here.

Tragedy struck on October 5, 1916, during a fire at Christian Brothers College at Kingshighway and Easton Avenue. Firefighters were operating on the third floor when a collapse occurred, taking the lives of six firefighters and three civilians. Five of those killed were from Hook and Ladder 19—Lieutenant Michael Waters, Fireman William Kuhnert, Fireman John Parshall, Fireman August Sturmfels, and Fireman George Young. Lieutenant Harry Budde of Engine Company 43 was also killed.

During the 1942 reorganization of the fire department, Engine Company 50 was taken out of service and replaced by Engine Company 18.

In 1975, Engine 18 was taken out of service. The station was closed and torn down a short time later. Note the relatively small apparatus bay door opening and the ornate lighting on the outside of the building.

FIRE STATION 51

4300 Eichelberger Street

This station opened in 1910 for Engine Company 51 and has the distinction of being the last to be assigned horse-drawn companies when new. During the restructuring of the department in 1942, Engine Company 51 was taken out of service and replaced by Engine Company 19. The station closed in 1956 when Engine Company 19 moved to a new station at 6624 Morgan Ford (then known as Morganford) Road where they continue to operate today. The station on Eichelberger was razed a short time after.

FIRE STATION 52

6810 Clayton Avenue

Situated on the west side of St. Louis, this station opened on December 11, 1911, with Engine Company 52 and Hook and Ladder 18. On April 17, 1922, while responding to an alarm, Engine Company 52's 1911 Webb 700-GPM pumper collided with City Limits streetcar #68 at the intersection of Forsyth Boulevard and Skinker Boulevard, killing Lieutenant Michael Kane, Fireman Eugene Carten, and Fireman John Haas.

In 1942, Engine Company 52 was taken out of service and replaced by Engine Company 22. This station was closed in 1957 due to the construction of Highway 40. The companies moved into a new station only a half mile away at 1229 McCausland Avenue.

FIRE STATION 53

5245 Natural Bridge Avenue

This station opened on April 16, 1922, with Engine Company 53 and operated as such until 1942 when they were taken out of service and replaced with Engine Company 24. Engine Company 24 continues to operate at this station today.

FIRE STATION 54

4520 Margaretta Avenue

Engine Company 54 and Hook and Ladder Company 21 operated at this station, which opened on June 1, 1917. From 1933 to 1942, Inhalator Company 4 also was stationed here.

In 1942, Engine Company 54 was taken out of service and replaced by Engine Company 26. Hook and Ladder 21 was taken out of service in 1975 and became Hook and Ladder 9, operating here until 1986. Today, Engine Company 26 and Medic 26 respond from this station. Note the small addition framed out on the left side of the second floor.

FIRE STATION 55

5435 Partridge Avenue

St. Louis paid $27,440.80 to construct Fire Station 55.

This building opened in September 1922 for Engine Company 55 and Hook and Ladder Company 20. It faces south at the wedge of Riverview Boulevard and Partridge Avenue. In 1942, Engine Company 55 was permanently taken out of service, with Engine Company 27 assigned here. In 1975, Hook and Ladder Company 20 became Hook and Ladder 7, which they continued as until being taken out of service in 1986. Today, Truck 27 and Marine Unit 4 operate from this station.

FIRE STATION 56

5000 South Kingshighway at Christy Boulevard

This station opened on April 1, 1926, with Engine Company 56 and Hook and Ladder Company 23. This station's opening marked the time of the highest number of stations and companies in the St. Louis Fire Department.

In 1942, Engine Company 56 was taken out of service in and replaced by Engine Company 36. Hook and Ladder 23 was taken out of service in 1975 and replaced by Hook and Ladder 4. Today, the station is operated by Truck Company 36 and Hook and Ladder 3. Note the proud firefighters and their apparatus posed in front of their station shortly after it opened. The station is arguably one of the most beautiful in St. Louis.

CK CO. NO. 1
ENGINE CO.

OTHER FIRE DEPARTMENT FACILITIES

1904 WORLD'S FAIR FIRE STATION 4

World Fair Fairgrounds–Forest Park

The World's Fair was held in St. Louis in 1904. The fairgrounds were located on the western edge of St. Louis and saw the construction of many buildings. The St. Louis Fire Department had a large presence on-site, with apparatus assigned to four different locations. This photo shows Fire Station 4, which was assigned newly formed Engine Company 42, Hook and Ladder 14, and Chemical Company 1. They operated on-site until the fair closed, when they were moved to other stations. This station was closed and torn down.

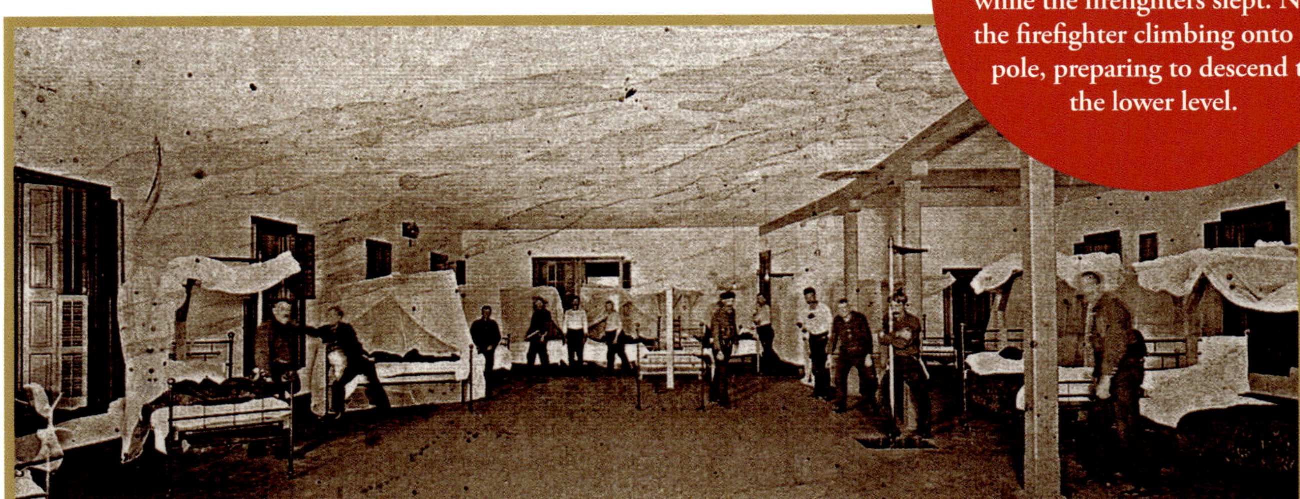

Photo showing the bunk hall of the station. It is believed that the mesh around the beds was to keep bugs away while the firefighters slept. Note the firefighter climbing onto the pole, preparing to descend to the lower level.

FIRE DEPARTMENT HORSE HOSPITAL

2408 North Twenty-Second Street

Prior to motorized vehicles, fire apparatus were first pulled to the scene by men and later by horses. The St. Louis Fire Department relied on horses for more than fifty years to get their apparatus to the scene. Part of that reliance included caring for the horses, preparing them for their service, and caring for them when they were sick or injured. This building served as the horse hospital and was located adjacent to a warehouse between it and Fire Station 5. This building remained standing for many years after the horses were gone but later was torn down. Note the horse head cast in the wall at the top of the building.

FIRE DEPARTMENT REPAIR SHOP

2004 Washington Avenue

In the above photo showing Engine Company 32 on the ramp of their station, the two-bay structure to the right is the Fire Department Repair Shop. It was first constructed in 1902 with a second floor added in 1904. In 1919, Engine Company 32 was moved to a different station, and the repair shop took over their quarters. In 1929, a new repair shop was constructed at 1125 Spruce Street, and this building was closed. The repair shop portion of this building was razed, but the old fire station remains standing today and is home to the Brick River Cider Company.

Photo taken in the 1920s showing the staff assigned to the repair shop.

FIRE DEPARTMENT REPAIR SHOP AND TRAINING SCHOOL

1125 Spruce Street

This building opened on January 27, 1929, and was located behind Fire Station 14–24 at 314 South Twelfth Street. Presently known as Fire Station 2, the school was relocated to the new Fire Department Headquarters on December 27, 1988. The repair shop operated into the middle of the first decade of the twenty-first century when services were contracted for several years to Metro. The fire department occupied a new repair shop in 2018, and these facilities are currently used for storage.

The Civil Defense set up a temporary training school located at 4605 DeTonty to train firefighters in structural collapse and other rescue scenarios.

LAMBERT–ST. LOUIS INTERNATIONAL AIRPORT

Crash-Fire-Rescue Station

This is the only known photo showing the station operated by the St. Louis Fire Department from 1958 to 1963. It was located at the end of Missouri Air National Guard Hanger #1.

LAMBERT–ST. LOUIS INTERNATIONAL AIRPORT

Crash-Fire-Rescue Station

This station opened in 1963 and was the lone fire station operating at Lambert until 1984 when a new structure was constructed on the north side of the runways. At that time, this became known as the Remote Station, which operated into the twenty-first century before closing. It is presently used for storage.

UNDERWRITERS SALVAGE CORPS
AGE CORPS

ST. LOUIS UNDERWRITERS SALVAGE CORPS

UNDERWRITERS SALVAGE CORPS SALVAGE HOUSE 1

711 Locust Street

The Underwriters Salvage Corps had a large presence in the city of St. Louis for many years, dating to 1874. They operated from a number of stations including this one built in 1884. This station operated until 1903 when the company moved to a new station several blocks west.

It is unknown if the company occupied the entire building or just the lower level with the apparatus bays.

UNDERWRITERS SALVAGE CORPS SALVAGE HOUSE 1

1127 Locust Street

The Salvage Corps operated this station from 1903 to 1918. Note the decorations and "welcome" sign on the building, presumably celebrating an open house.

UNDERWRITERS SALVAGE CORPS SALVAGE HOUSE 1

1211 Pine Street

The Salvage Corps operated this station from 1918 to 1947. It was initially occupied by Salvage 1, with Salvage 2 and 3 both moving in during 1938. This station closed in 1947 with the companies moving to the station at 3321 Locust Street.

UNDERWRITERS SALVAGE CORPS SALVAGE HOUSE 2

1310 Merchant Street

The Salvage Corps operated this station from 1887 to 1916.

Charles Evans, the first Chief of the Salvage Corps, directed the construction of this station.

UNDERWRITERS SALVAGE CORPS SALVAGE HOUSE 2

2310 Sidney Street

The Salvage Corps operated this station from 1916 to 1938. At that time, the company moved to Salvage House 1.

This building remained standing for many years and once operated as one of St. Louis's well-known O. T. Hodge Chile Company parlors. This building has since been razed.

UNDERWRITERS SALVAGE CORPS SALVAGE HOUSE 3

3321 Locust Street

The Salvage Corps operated Company 3 from this station starting in 1893. In 1920, a new front was added to the station with Salvage 3 temporarily moving to St. Louis Fire Station 28 at 3934 Enright Avenue. In 1938, this station closed, and Salvage Company 3 moved to Station 1.

UNDERWRITERS SALVAGE CORPS SALVAGE HOUSE 3

3321 Locust Street

The Salvage Corps reopened Company 3 in 1941. This photo shows the building with the new addition completed in 1920. In 1947, both companies from Salvage 1 and 2 moved into this station.

At midnight on December 31, 1955, the Underwriters Salvage Corps disbanded after serving the city of St. Louis since 1874. This building is still standing and is used as a personal residence.

FIRE
STATION
7-32
LOUIS
HOOK & LADDER
Nº 8

PRESENT STATIONS

(AS PHOTOGRAPHED DURING THE 1960s AND 1970s)

FIRE STATION 1

2910 South Jefferson Avenue

Located in the Benton Park neighborhood, this station opened in 1975 for Engine Companies 1 and 3 as well as Rescue Squad 1. In 1981, Engine Company 3 was taken out of service.

Today, the station is occupied by Engine Company 1, Rescue Squad Company 1 and the Collapse Rescue Task Force including Units 852 and 853, and a tractor-trailer USAR unit. In addition to the fire department personnel assigned to Station 1, a mask service repair facility also operates here.

FIRE STATION 2

314 South Twelfth Street
(formerly Fire Station 14–24)

This station opened in 1929 for Engine Companies 14 and 24 along with Rescue Squad 1. In 1933, Water Tower I and Foam Truck 2 moved in. During the restructuring of companies that occurred in 1941–42, Engine Company 2 moved into this station as did Hook and Ladder 6, Hose Wagon 1 in 1942 (through 1971), and Foam Truck 1 in 1943 (through 1956). At the same time, Engine Companies 14 and 24, Rescue Squad 1, Water Tower 1, and Foam 2 all relocated to different stations.

Rescue Squad 2 was assigned here from 1965 to 1974.

This photo shows the station as constructed. The facing page includes a photo of the station after modifications.

FIRE STATION 2

314 South Tucker Boulevard
(formerly South Twelfth Street)
(formerly Station 14–24)

This photo of the station shows it after the construction of two additional apparatus bays on the south side of the building in 1966.

After the construction, Snorkel 1 replaced Hook and Ladder 6 and operated until 1975 when its designation was changed to Snorkel 6. Engine Company 15 operated from the station briefly from 1978 to 1981 and then was taken out of service.

Apparatus presently assigned to the station are Engine Company 2, Hook and Ladder 2, Chemical Unit 1, Medic 2, and Battalion Chief 802.

FIRE STATION 4

4425 South Compton Avenue (formerly Station 44)

This station opened in 1906 as Station 44 with its designation changing to Station 4 in 1942. At the time, Engine Company 4 and Hook and Ladder 16 were assigned here. Hook and Ladder 16 was taken out of service in 1976. In 1986 and 1987, Hook and Ladder 14 operated at this station.

The building was remodeled in 1990 and today is home to Truck Company 4 and Battalion Chief 804 serving the Dutchtown neighborhood.

FIRE STATION 5

2123 North Market Street (formerly Station 5–25)

This large station opened in 1953 for Engine Companies 5 and 25, Hook and Ladder 2, and Hose Wagon 4. Hose Wagon 4 was taken out of service in 1971 as was Engine Company 25. Rescue Squad 2 ran out of this station from 1978 to 1986, and Fuel Truck 1 was also assigned here. In 1999, Medic 5 was assigned here, and in 2009 Hook and Ladder 2 was re-designated Hook and Ladder 1 to coincide with the district they were assigned to.

Today, the station serves the St. Louis Place neighborhood and is assigned Truck 5, Hook and Ladder 1, Medic 5, and Battalion Chief 801.

1971 Seagrave pumper assigned to Engine 5, equipped with a 1500–GPM pump and 300-gallon tank

Photo taken in the mid-1980s when a Pumper 6 and Hook and Ladder 10 were assigned here shows the tight quarters and original apparatus bay door. This beautiful arched doorway was replaced shortly thereafter to accommodate larger modern apparatus.

FIRE STATION 6

5747 Manchester Avenue
(formerly Station 42)

This station opened in 1905 for Engine Company 42. On April 2, 1975, Engine Company 42 was taken out of service and Engine Company 6 was reorganized here. Engine Company 6 continues their service here today protecting the Cheltenham neighborhood.

FIRE STATION 7

2600 LaSalle Street (formerly Station 7–32)

The station opened in 1971 and was assigned Engine Companies 7 and 32, Hook and Ladder 8, and Battalion Chief 8. In 1974, Engine Company 32 moved to the station located at 3500 South Grand and was replaced by Engine Company 18 in 1975. In 1978, Engine Company 18 was permanently taken out of service, and Hook and Ladder 8 was taken out of service in 1986. Other companies assigned to the station over the years included Deputy Chief 810, Battalion Chief 802, and Fuel Truck 1.

Today, the station is occupied by Truck 7, Fire Investigative Unit 821, and the St. Louis City Unified Command unit. It serves the Gate District neighborhood.

FIRE STATION 8

1501 Salisbury Street

This station opened in 1928 to replace the former station at the same site that was badly damaged by a tornado. This station featured a partial basement in the rear of the building under the captain's room that contained a furnace. In 1986, the furnace was relocated and the basement was filled in. The engine room floor was lowered to accommodate the 1987 Pierce Arrow with a 50-foot Tele-Squrt when the Total Quint Concept was implemented.

Engine Company 8 continues to operate from the station in Hyde Park today.

FIRE STATION 9

814 La Beaume Street

This station opened in 1957, and Engine Company 9 and Hook and Ladder 7 first operated here. Over the years, a number of companies have been assigned to this station including Foam Truck 1 from 1962 to 1964 and Foam Truck 3 from 1969 to 1975, when they were redesignated Foam Truck 1 and continued here until 1978. Hook and Ladder 7 was taken out of service in 1974, and Rescue Squad 2 served here from 1974 to 1978. In 1978, Engine Company 25 and Hook and Ladder 13 were assigned here but only operated until 1981 when both were taken out of service. In 1999, Medic 14 was assigned to the station and redesignated Medic 9.

Today, Engine Company 9 and Medic 9 occupy this station, providing protection in the primarily industrial area known as the Near North Riverfront neighborhood. Note the small room on the right side of the building, which serves as the Joker Room.

Opened on February 27, 1957, Fire Station 9 was built for $162,484.

FIRE STATION 10

4161 Kennerly Avenue (formerly Station 46)

This station opened on March 14, 1908, as Station 46. Engine Company 46 was taken out of service in 1942, and Engine Company 10 and Hose Wagon 12 were assigned here. The hose wagon moved out in 1949, and Engine Company 10 operated as the lone company at this station for fifty years until Medic 11 moved in during 1999.

From 1945 to 1961, this was one of several fire stations in St. Louis operated by all black firefighters.

Today, Truck 10 and Medic 10 protect the residents of the Ville neighborhood from this busy station. If you look closely at the photo, you can see the "46" behind the "10."

FIRE STATION 11

2224 South Seventh Street (formerly Station 11–16)

This station opened in 1963 for Engine Companies 11 and 16 with Hook and Ladder 1 moving in during 1971. In 1973, Foam Company 7 was assigned here, and it was redesignated Foam Company 2 in 1975. Engine Company 16 was taken out of service in 1981, and Hook and Ladder 1, the last tractor-trailer/tillered ladder operated in St. Louis, was taken out of service in 1985.

Today, the station is occupied by Truck 11 and the Marine Unit Task Force protecting the Kosciusko neighborhood. In addition to the various apparatus assigned to the station, it is equipped with one of several commercial extractors owned by the fire department, which is used to clean turnout gear.

FIRE STATION 12

5214 West Florissant Avenue (formerly Station 47)

This station opened in 1909 as Fire Station 47. During restructuring of the department in 1942, Engine Company 47 was taken out of service and Engine Company 12 was assigned here along with Hose Wagon 11. Other companies operating here over the years included Gasoline Supply Truck 5, District Chief 11, Battalion Chief 6, as well as Hook and Ladder 7 from 1986 to 1987.

Medic 6 was assigned here in 1999, redesignated Medic 12, and operated until 2009 when they were reassigned to Station 26.

Today Hook and Ladder 6, reactivated in 2009, operates as the sole company from this station protecting the Mark Twain neighborhood.

FIRE STATION 13

1400 Shawmut Place (formerly Station 48)

This station opened in 1909 for Engine Company 48 and Hook and Ladder 17. During the restructuring of the department in 1942, Engine Company 48 was taken out of service and Engine Company 13 replaced them at this station. Hose Wagon 10 joined the two companies here, operating from 1946 to 1971. In 1976, Hook and Ladder 17 was renumbered Hook and Ladder 3. They operated here until the implementation of the Total Quint Concept in 1987 when Hook and Ladder 3 was taken out of service. Medic 7 moved to Station 13 in 1999 and was renumbered Medic 13.

In the first decade of the twenty-first century, renovations to the interior of this beautiful station included a number of the windows being bricked in. Today, the station is home to Truck 13 and Medic 13, which provide protection to the residents of the Hamilton Heights neighborhood.

FIRE STATION 14

3523 Magnolia Avenue (formerly Station 49)

This station opened in 1909 for Engine Company 49. During the restructuring of the department in 1942, Engine Company 49 was taken out of service and Engine Company 14 called this station home along with Hook and Ladder 14. In 1976, Hook and Ladder 14 moved to Station 32, and in 1999 Medic 3 moved to the station and was renumbered Medic 14. Today Engine 14 and Medic 14 call this station home and protect the residents and visitors to the Tower Grove East neighborhood.

Note how the front of the station has changed with the removal of the concrete work above the roofline and an overgrowth of trees in front of the station when compared to the photo on page 65 when the station was new.

FIRE STATION 17

3238 Martin Luther King Drive

This station opened in 1925 for Engine Company 17, Hook and Ladder 22, which was organized at the station, and District Chief 6.

In 1974, District Chief 6 relocated to a different station, and Hook and Ladder 22 was taken out of service.

Today, Truck 17 calls the station home in the Covenant Blue/Grand Center neighborhood.

Photo of Engine 17's 1950 Mack 1000-GPM pumper and Hook and Ladder 22's 65-foot aerial

FIRE STATION 19

6624 Morgan Ford Road

This station opened in 1956 for Engine Company 19. The construction of the station fits nicely with the homes in the neighborhood. Today the 19s provide protection to those in the Boulevard Heights neighborhood. Note Morganford on the street sign. Today known as Morgan Ford it has long been the subject of local debate.

FIRE STATION 20

5600 Prescott Avenue

This new station opened in 1960 for Engine Company 20, Hook and Ladder 12, and Hose Wagon 7. In 1971, Hose Wagon 7 was taken out of service, and Foam Truck 7 was assigned here. They operated until 1975 when they were renumbered Foam Truck 1.

Today, Truck 20 and Battalion Chief 806 are assigned to this station, which is located in the North Riverfront neighborhood.

FIRE STATION 22

1229 McCausland Avenue

This station opened in 1958 just a short distance from the former Station 22, which was closed to make room for the construction of Highway 40 running through St. Louis. At the time, Engine Company 22 and Hook and Ladder 18 were assigned here. In 1960, Hose Wagon 9 moved in and operated until 1971. Hook and Ladder 18 was taken out of service in 1976 and replaced by Hook and Ladder 16, which operated until 1985 when they were permanently removed from service.

Photo of the basement of Station 22 when the Mask Service Unit was operating here

Medic 12 was assigned to the station in 1999 and renumbered Medic 22 but only operated here until 2000 when they were relocated to Station 29. At one time, the Mask Service Unit was located in the basement of Station 22 and took care of service and repair of the department's SCBAs. The current station is located right alongside Interstate 64 and is home to Truck 22 serving the Hi-Pointe neighborhood.

FIRE STATION 23

6500 Michigan Avenue

Fire Station 23 opened in 1921 for Engine Company 23, Hook and Ladder 11, Fuel Wagon 5, and District Chief 10. Over the years, the Fuel Wagon and District Chief were moved to other stations, and Hook and Ladder 11 was removed from service in 1986. Medic 1 moved to this station in 1999 and was renumbered Medic 23.

Today, Engine Company 23 and Medic 23 protect the residents and businesses in the Carondelet neighborhood on the city's south side. This station has the distinction of being the only one in St. Louis to have roman numerals for the company number above the apparatus door. This photo shows the station after modifications were made to accommodate modern apparatus.

FIRE STATION 24

5245 Natural Bridge Avenue (formerly Fire Station 53)

This station was built in 1922 for Engine Company 53. During the restructuring of the department in 1942, Engine Company 53 was taken out of service and was replaced by Engine Company 24.

Today, Engine Company 24 operates from the station located in the Mark Twain/I-70 Industrial neighborhood.

This photo shows the 24's 1987 Pierce Arrow pumper equipped with a 50-foot Tele-Squrt, part of the first wave of quints utilized for the Total Quint Concept.

FIRE STATION 26

4520 Margaretta Avenue (formerly Fire Station 54)

This station opened in 1917 for Engine Company 54 and newly organized Hook and Ladder 21. Engine Company 54 was removed from service in 1942 and replaced by Engine Company 26. In 1975, Hook and Ladder 21 was renumbered Hook and Ladder 9 but only operated until 1986 when they were taken out of service.

Medic 12 was assigned to this station in 2010 and renumbered Medic 26 in 2014. Located in the Penrose neighborhood, today this station is occupied by Engine Company 26 and Medic 26.

Note the 1957 American LaFrance pumper and 1944 Seagrave ladder in the station.

FIRE STATION 27

5435 Partridge Avenue
(formerly Fire Station 55)

This station opened in 1922 for Engine Company 55 and Hook and Ladder 20. In 1942, Engine Company 55 was taken out of service and replaced by Engine Company 27. In 1975, Hook and Ladder 20 was taken out of service and replaced by Hook and Ladder 7, which operated here until 1986.

Situated in the Walnut Park East neighborhood, Fire Station 27 is presently home to Truck 27 and Marine Unit 4.

Photo of 1924 General–St. Louis service truck assigned to Hook and Ladder 20

1951 Mack L 1000-GPM with 200-gallon tank

FIRE STATION 28

4810 Enright Avenue
(formerly Fire Station 43)

This station was constructed in 1932 and first occupied by Engine Company 43 and Hook and Ladder 15. In 1975, Engine Company 43 was taken out of service, and Engine Company 28 moved into the station. After the change, this station was also used by Battalion Chief 5 and DeCon Unit 1. In 2009, Hook and Ladder 15 was renumbered Hook and Ladder 5 to reflect the district in which they were stationed.

The station is located in the Fountain Park neighborhood, and Engine Company 28, Hook and Ladder 5, Battalion Chief 5, and the HazMat Task Force are assigned here.

FIRE STATION 29

200 South Vandeventer Avenue
(formerly Fire Station 21)

This station opened in 1965 for Engine Companies 21 and 29, Hook and Ladder 5, Rescue Squad 1, and Battalion Chief 7. Rescue Squad 1 moved after only a year and was replaced by Hose Wagon 12, which moved in and operated until 1971.

In 1972, Hook and Ladder 5 was taken out of service and replaced by Snorkel Company 2. They were changed to Snorkel 5 in 1975 and operated here until 1986 when they were taken out of service. At that time, Rescue Squad 2 moved to the station. Other companies assigned here included:

- Foam Truck 3 (1992–1994)
- Foam Truck 4 (1994–2004)
- Medic 29 (2000–2011)

Today, this station located in Midtown St. Louis is home to Engine Company 29, Rescue Squad 2, and Hazardous Material Unit 3.

1960 Mack C95F-1089 1000-GPM pumper with 300-gallon tank

FIRE STATION 30

541 DeBaliviere Avenue

This station opened in 1957 as the new quarters for Engine Company 30.

Today, Truck Company 30 occupies the station, which is located in the Skinker/DeBaliviere neighborhood just north of Forest Park.

Firefighters train with their 1951 Mack L 750-GPM pumper.

FIRE STATION 31

4408 Donovan Avenue

Fire Station 31 opened in 1953 for Engine Company 31. Other companies assigned here included Hose Wagon 9 from 1958 to 1960 and Hook and Ladder 4 from 1969 to 1971. In 1999, Medic 2 moved to this station and was renumbered Medic 31.

Today, Fire Station 31 is occupied by Engine Company 31 and Medic 31, protecting the beautiful homes of St. Louis Hills.

FIRE STATION 32

3500 South Grand Avenue
(formerly Fire Station 38)

This station was constructed in 1899 for Engine Company 38. In 1975, Engine Company 32 moved into the station, and they operated together for about a year when Engine 38 was taken out of service and Engine 33 moved in. The 33s moved out in 1976 when Hook and Ladder 14 was assigned here. They operated until 1986 when they were taken out of service. In 1999, Medic 4 moved in and was renumbered Medic 32.

Today, the station retains much of its original character and is home to Engine Company 32 and Medic 32 serving the Tower Grove East neighborhood.

FIRE STATION 33

8300 North Broadway
(formerly Fire Station 37)

This station was built in 1909 for Engine Company 37, with Hook and Ladder 3 joining them in 1933. Both units operated here until 1976 when they were taken out of service and replaced by Engine Company 33.

Medic 8 moved into this station in 1999 and was renumbered Medic 33.

Today, this station in the Baden area of St. Louis is home to Engine Company 33 and Medic 33.

Hook and Ladder 3's 1956 American LaFrance 85-foot tiller

FIRE STATION 34

8227 South Broadway

This station opened on November 12, 1895, for Engine Company 34 and has the distinction of being the oldest continuously occupied fire station in the St. Louis Fire Department. Today, Truck 34 responds from here protecting the Patch neighborhood.

FIRE STATION 35

5450 Arsenal Street

This station opened in 1895 for Engine Company 35 and Hook and Ladder 10.

In 1959–1960, the front of the station was remodeled to accommodate a new bay door and give it a more modern appearance. (Some are of the opinion that those efforts ruined the historical character and beauty of the station, as shown on page 54.)

Hook and Ladder 10 was taken out of service in 1987. In 1999, Medic 9 was assigned to the station and renumbered Medic 35.

Today, the station located in the Southwest Garden neighborhood is home to Truck 35, Medic 35, and Battalion Chief 803, whose quarters are located at the rear of the structure.

FIRE STATION 36

5000 South Kingshighway Boulevard
(formerly Fire Station 56)

This station was built in 1926 for Engine Company 56 and Hook and Ladder 23. In 1942, Engine Company 56 was replaced by Engine Company 36, which operated with Hook and Ladder 23 until 1974 when their designation was changed to Hook and Ladder 4. In 2012, the designation was changed again, this time to Hook and Ladder 3 to represent the district they are located in.

A tragedy occurred on September 18, 1955, when four firefighters from Engine Company 36 were killed in a collision with a tractor-trailer at Manchester and Kingshighway when they were moving up to Fire Station 18.

Today, this Princeton Heights neighborhood station is home to Truck 36 and Hook and Ladder 3.

VOLUNTEER STATIONS

Station	Address	Dates Occupied	Occupied By	Structure
Central Fire Company 1	West side of Main, south of Market	1832–18XX	Central Fire Company 1	First Location, Frame Structure
Central Fire Company 1	South side of Chestnut, between 3rd and 4th Streets	18XX–1859	Central Fire Company 1	Second Location, Brick Structure
Union Fire Company 2	East side of 3rd, north of Washington	1832–18XX	Union Fire Company 2	First Location, Frame Shed
Union Fire Company 2	West side of 3rd, south of Washington	18XX–1855	Union Fire Company 2 and Lafayette Hook & Ladder	Second Location, Brick Structure
Washington Fire Company 3	East side of 2nd, south of Spruce	1833–18XX	Washington Fire Company 3	First Location, Frame Structure
Washington Fire Company 3	South side of Spruce, between 2nd and 3rd	18XX–18XX	Washington Fire Company 3	Second Location, Brick Structure
Washington Fire Company 3	West side of 3rd, between Elm and Clark	18XX–1857	Washington Fire Company 3	Third Location, Brick Structure
St. Louis Fire Company 4	Northwest corner of 4th and Locust	1839–18XX	St. Louis Fire Company 4	First Location, Frame Shed
St. Louis Fire Company 4	Southwest corner of 3rd and Locust	18XX–1859	St. Louis Fire Company 4	Second Location, Brick Structure
Missouri Fire Company 5	Northwest corner of 4th and Locust	1839–1852	Missouri Fire Company 5	First Location, Frame Shed
Missouri Fire Company 5	Southwest corner of 3rd and Olive	1852–18XX	Missouri Fire Company 5	Second Location, Frame Structure
Missouri Fire Company 5	East side of 3rd, below Olive	18XX–18XX	Missouri Fire Company 5	Third Location, Brick Structure
Missouri Fire Company 5	East side of 3rd, south of Olive	18XX–1859	Missouri Fire Company 5	Fourth Location, Brick Structure
Liberty Fire Company 6	Southwest corner of 3rd and Franklin	1841–1858	Liberty Fire Company 6	Only Location, Brick Structure
Phoenix Fire Company 7	Apex of 2nd, 5th, and Park	1843–18XX	Phoenix Fire Company 7	First Location, Frame Structure
Phoenix Fire Company 7	West side of Broadway, north of Park	18XX–1858	Phoenix Fire Company 7	Second Location, Brick Structure
Franklin Fire Company 8	Northwest corner of Franklin and 11th	1844–1848	Franklin Fire Company 8	First Location, Frame Shed
Franklin Fire Company 8	West side of 11th, between Washington and Carr	1848–1857	Franklin Fire Company 8	Second Location, Frame Structure
Mound Fire Company 9	South side of Howard, east of Broadway	1847–1852	Mound Fire Company 9	First Location, Frame Structure
Mound Fire Company 9	West side of Broadway, south of Brooklyn	1852–1857	Mound Fire Company 9	Second Location, Brick Structure
Laclede Fire Company 10	North side of Market, east of 15th	1848–1858	Laclede Fire Company 10	
South Saint Louis Volunteer Fire Company	South side of Allen, between 7th and 8th	1856–1857	South Saint Louis Volunteer Fire Company	
Jefferson Volunteer Fire Company	South side of Franklin, between 22nd and 23rd	1856–1857	Jefferson Volunteer Fire Company	
North Saint Louis Volunteer Fire Dept.	Broadway and Angelrodt	1857	North Saint Louis Volunteer Fire Department	Not associated with St. Louis Volunteer Fire Dept.
Good Will Volunteer Fire Company 11	North side of Market, west of Broadway	1858	Good Will Volunteer Fire Company 11	Rented quarters from disbanded company

PAID STATIONS

Station	Address	Dates Occupied	Occupied By	Former/Became
1	1015 North 11th	1857–1874	Engine 1 (1857–1874)	Former Franklin Fire Company 8
1	2411 McNair	1874–1971	Engine 1 (1874–1971), Hook & Ladder 1 (1877–1971), District Chief 8 (1896–?)	Private Residence
1–3	2910 South Jefferson	1975 –1981	Engine 1, Engine 3, and Rescue Squad 1 (All units 1975–1981)	Became Station 1
1		1981–Present	Engine 1, Rescue Squad 1, Collapse–Rescue Task Force 852 & 853, STARRS USAR Unit Strike Force 2, Mask Service Repair	In Service
2	720 Washington	1857–1859	Engine 2 (1857–1859), Fuel Cart	Became Station 5
2	2218 Franklin	1859–1871	Engine 2 (1859–1871)	Former Franklin Fire Company 8
2	129 West Krause	1871–1903	Engine 2 (1871–1903), Fuel Wagon 5 (1877), Addition–1882, Chemical & Ladder 2 (1883–1895), Hook & Ladder 11 (1895–1921)	Became Station 23
2	508 North 3rd	1903–1941	Engine 2, Hook & Ladder 6	Razed
2	314 South 12th	1941–1966	Engine 2, Hook & Ladder 6, and Hose Wagon 2 (All 1942–1966), Foam 1 (1943–1956), Foam 2 (1956–1962), Rescue 2 (1965)	
2	1966 Addition	1966–Present	Engine 2, Engine 15 (1978–1981), Snorkel 1 (1966–1975), Snorkel 6 (1975–1986), Hose Wagon 2 (1966–1971), Rescue 2 (1966–1974), Hook & Ladder 6 (1986–2009), Hook & Ladder 2 (2009–Present), Foam Truck 4 (2004–2018), Battalion Chief 802, Medic 2, Chemical Unit 1 (2020)	In Service
3	211 South 3rd	1857–1863	Engine 3 (1857–1863)	Former Washington Fire Company 3
3	415 South 5th (Broadway)	1863–1874	Engine 3 (1864–1874), Fuel Wagon 2 (1868–1885), Hook & Ladder 1 (1872–1877)	Became Station 15–39
3	3648 South Broadway (Orig.)	1874–1918	Engine 3 (1874–1918), Fuel Wagon 4	Razed
3	3648 South Broadway	1919–1969	Engine 3 (1919–1969), Gasoline Supply Truck 4	Owned by St. Louis
1–3	2910 South Jefferson	1975 –1981	Engine 1, Engine 3, and Rescue Squad 1 (All units 1975–1981)	Became Station 1
4	2233 Cole Street	1871–1933	Engine 4 (1871–1933), Water Tower 1 (1931–1933)	Former General Lyon Volunteer Company
4	4425 South Compton	1942–Present	Engine Company 4 (1942–2011), Hook & Ladder 16 (1942–1976), Hook & Ladder 14 (1986–1987), Battalion Chief 10, Battalion Chief 4, Truck 4 (2011–Present)	Former Station 44 In Service
5	216 North 7th	1858–1859	Engine 5 (1858–1859)	Former Missouri Fire Company 5
5	216 North 7th	1869–1874	Engine 5, Hook & Ladder 2	
5	1800 North Market	1873–1887	Engine 5, Hook & Ladder 2	Conflicting information regarding the existence of this station
5	2400 North 22nd	1874–1953	Engine 5, Hook & Ladder 2	Warehouse storage for fire alarm
5–25	2123 North Market	1953–1971	Engine 5, Engine 25, Hook & Ladder 2, Hose Wagon 4 (All units 1953–1971)	Became Station 5
5	2123 North Market	1971–Present	Engine 5 (1971–2011), Truck 5 (2011–Present), Hook & Ladder 2 (1971–2009), Hook & Ladder 1 (2009–Present), Rescue Squad 2 (1978–1986), Fuel Truck 1, Medic 5 (1999–Present), Battalion Chief 801	In Service
6	South Side Allen, 7th & 8th	1857–1858	Engine 6	Former South Saint Louis Volunteer Fire Company
6	1337 South Broadway	1858–1874	Engine 6 (1858–1874)	Former Phoenix Fire Company 7
6	216 North 7th	1874–1902	Engine 6, Hook & Ladder 3, Fuel Wagon 1, and FD Headquarters	Former Missouri Fire Company 5 and SLFD Station 5
6	12 North 9th	1902–1939	Engine 6, Hook & Ladder 3 (1902–1933) Closed for remodeling, 1939–1941	Razed
6	12 North 9th (Remodeled)	1941–1965	Engine 6, Hook & Ladder 6 (1941–1942), Gas Truck 1 and Foam Truck 1 (1942–1943), Canteen (1944–1954), Rescue Squad 1 (1943–1965)	Razed
6	5747 Manchester (MO Hwy. 100)	1975–Present	Engine 6 (1975–2011), Hook & Ladder 10 (1986–1987), Truck 6 (2011–2018), Engine 6 (2018–Present)	Former Station 42
7	1425 Market	1858–1873	Engine 7	Former Laclede Fire Company 10
7	1304 South 18th	1873–1896	Engine 7	Destroyed by Tornado, 1896
7	1304 South 18th	1897–1971	Engine 7, Hook & Ladder 14 (1905–1942), Hose Wagon 5 (1942–1971), District Chief 3, Engine 33 (1963–1965)	Private Residence
7–32	2600 LaSalle	1971–1974	Engine 7, Engine 32, Hook & Ladder 8 (Aerialscope 8)	Became Station 7
7	2600 LaSalle	1974–Present	Engine 7 (1974–2011), Truck 7 (2011–Present), Engine 18 (1975–1978), Hook & Ladder 8 (1974–1986), Fuel Truck 1, Deputy Chief 810 (19XX–19XX), Battalion Chief 802 (19XX–19XX), Fire Investigative Unit 821, St. Louis Unified Command Post	In Service
8	1501 Salisbury (Orig.)	1865–1927	Engine 8	Destroyed by tornado
8	1501 Salisbury	1928–Present	Engine 8, Battalion Chief 5 (19XX), Basement filled/floor lowered in 1986	In Service
9	2400 South 4th	1867–1871	Engine 9	Became Station 11
9	Broadway, south of Brooklyn	1871–1885	Engine 9 (1871–1885)	Former Mound Fire Company 9 and SLFD Station 4

PAID STATIONS

Station	Address	Dates Occupied	Occupied By	Former/Became
9	1545 North 8th	1885–1957	Engine 9, Hook & Ladder 7, Water Tower 2 (1942–1957), Foam Truck (1955–1956), Foam Truck 1 (1956–1957)	Razed
9	814 La Beaume	1957–Present	Engine 9 (1957–2011), Engine 25 (1978–1981), Truck 9 (2011–2020), Engine 9 (2020), Hook & Ladder 7 (1957–1974), Hook & Ladder 13 (1978–1981) Foam 1 (1962–1964), Foam 2 (1969–1975), Foam 1 (1975–1978), Rescue 2 (1974–1978), Medic 9 (1999–Present)	In Service
10	20 South Jefferson (Orig.)	1867–1914	Engine 10	Razed
10	20 South Jefferson	1914–1942	Engine 10	Razed
10	4161 Kennerly	1942–Present	Engine 10 (1942–2011), Hose Wagon 12 (1942–1949), Hook & Ladder 9 (1960–1961), Truck 10 (2011–Present), Medic 10 (1999–Present)	Former Station 46
11	2400 South 4th (Orig.)	1871–1908	Engine 11	Former Station 9
11	2400 South 4th	1908–1963	Engine 11, Foam Truck 1 (1936–1942), Engine 45 (1939–1942), Hose Wagon 3 (1942–1949), Engine 16 (1961–1963)	Razed
11–16	2224 South 7th	1963–1981	Engine 11 and Engine 16 (1963–1981), Hook & Ladder 1 (1971–1981), Foam 7 (1973–1975), Foam 2 (1975–1981)	Became Station 11
11	2224 South 7th	1981–Present	Engine 11 (1981–2011), Truck 11 (2011–Present), Hook & Ladder 1 (1981–1985), Foam 2 (1981–20xx), Marine Unit Task Force	In Service
12–18	818 North 7th	1872–1939	Engines 12 (1872–1933) and 18 (1875–1939), Gasoline Supply Truck 6 (1928–1934), and FD Headquarters	Razed
12	5214 West Florissant	1942–Present	Engine 12 (1942–2009), Hose Wagon 11 (1942–1949), Battalion Chief 6, District Chief 11, Gasoline Supply Truck 5, Hook and Ladder 6 (2009–Present)	Former Station 47
13	1015 North 11th	1874–1933	Engine 13 (1874–1933)	Former Franklin Fire Company 8 and SLFD Station 1
13	1400 Shawmut	1942–Present	Engine 13 (1942–2011), Hook & Ladder 17 (1942–1976), Hook & Ladder 3 (1976–1987), Hose Wagon 10 (1946–1971), Truck 13 (2011–Present), Medic 13 (1999–Present)	Former Station 48
14	1425 Market	1873–1929	Engine 14	Former Franklin Fire Company 8 and SLFD Station 7
14–24	314 South 12th	1929–1942	Engine 14 (1929–1933), Engine 24 (1929–1942), Water Tower 1 (1933–1942), Rescue 1 (1934–1942), Foam 2 (1936–1942)	Became Station 2
14	3523 Magnolia	1942–Present	Engine 14 (1942–2011), Hook & Ladder 14 (Aerialscope 14) (1942–1976), Medic 14 (1999–Present), Truck 14 (2011–2020), Engine 14 (2020)	Former Station 49
15	415 South 5th (Broadway) (Orig.)	1874–1929	Engine 15 (1874–1929), Chemical 1 (1874–1900), Hook & Ladder 4 (1877–1929), Engine 39 (1900–1929)	Former Station 3
15–39	415 South Broadway (New)	1929–1969	Engine 15 (1929–1969), Engine 39 (1929–1960), Hook & Ladder 4 (1929–1963), Hose Wagon 1 (1929–1942), Snorkel 1(1963–1969), Foam 3 (1962–1969)	Razed for Busch Stadium
16	1337 South Broadway	1874–1961	Engine 16 (1874–1961)	Former Phoenix Fire Company 7 and SLFD Station 6
17	3220 Easton	1874–1925	Engine 17	Razed, 1925
17	3238 Martin Luther King (formerly Easton)	1925–Present	Engine 17 (1925–2011), Hook & Ladder 22 (1925–1974), District Chief 6 (1925–1974), Truck 17 (2011–Present)	In Service
12–18	818 North 7th	1872–1939	Engines 12 (1872–1933) and 18 (1875–1939), Gasoline Supply Truck 6 (1928–1934), and FD Headquarters	Razed
18	223 South Newstead	1942–1975	Engine 18 (1942–1975), Hook & Ladder 19 (1942–1975), Rescue Squad 1 (1974–1975)	Former Station 50
19	1120 St. Louis Avenue	1878–1933	Engine 19 (1878–1933), District Chief 5 (After being razed, lot became site of St. Louis Municipal Bath House No. 6.)	Razed
19	4300 Eichelberger	1942–1956	Engine 19 (1942–1956)	Former Station 51
19	6624 Morgan Ford	1956–Present	Engine 19 (1956–2011), Truck 19 (2011–2018), Engine 19 (2018–Present)	In Service
20	4551 North Broadway	1880–1960	Engine 20, addition in 1897 for Hook & Ladder 12 (1897–1960), Fuel Wagon 11, Gas Truck 3, Hose Wagon 7 (1942–1960)	Razed
20	5600 Prescott	1960–Present	Engine 20 (1960–2011), Hook & Ladder 12 (1960–1986), Hose Wagon 7 (1960–1971), Foam 7 (1971–1975), Foam 1 (1975–20XX), Truck 20 (2011–Present)	In service
21	3517 Market	1883–1928	Engine 21 (1883–1928), Hook & Ladder 5 (1883–1928), Fuel Supply Truck 1	Razed
21	3407 Market	1928–1965	Engine 21, Hook & Ladder 5, District Chief 7 (All 1928–1965), Foam Truck 2 (1943–1955)	Razed
21–29	200 South Vandeventer	1965–1978	Engine 21, Engine 29, Hook & Ladder 5 (1965–1972), Rescue 1 (1965–1966), Hose Wagon 12 (1966–1971), Battalion Chief 7 (1965–?)	Became Station 29
22	116 Plum Street	1885–1914	Engine 22, Fuel Wagon 2	Razed
22	831 South 6th	1914–1942	Engine 22, Gas Truck 8 (1914–1933)	Razed

PAID STATIONS

Station	Address	Dates Occupied	Occupied By	Former/Became
22	6810 Clayton	1942–1957	Engine 22, Hook & Ladder 18. Closed and razed in 1957 for construction of Highway 40.	Razed
22	1229 McCausland	1958–Present	Engine 22 (1958–2011), Hook & Ladder 18 (1958–1976), Hook & Ladder 16 (1976–1985), Hose Wagon 9 (1960–1971), Medic 22 (1999–2000), Truck 22 (2011–Present) (Mask Service Unit for SCBA repair in basement for several years)	In Service
23	508 North 3rd	1885–1903	Engine 23, Hook & Ladder 6, Chemical 3 (1885–1891), Water Tower 1 (1890–1896), and FD repair shop in basement (1885–1902)	Became Station 2
23	129 West Krause	1903–1921	Engine 23 (1903–1921), Hook & Ladder 11 (1895–1921)	Former Station 2
23	6500 Michigan	1921–Present	Engine 23, Hook & Ladder 11 (1921–1986), Fuel Wagon 5 (1921–19XX), District Chief 10 (1921–19XX), Medic 23 (1999–Present)	In Service
24	1214 Spruce	1884–1929	Engine 24 (In 1921 became first company with black firefighters)	Razed
14–24	314 South 12th	1929–1942	Engine 14 (1929–1933), Engine 24 (1929–1942), Water Tower 1 (1933–1942), Rescue 1 (1934–1942), Foam 2 (1936–1942)	Became Station 2
24	5245 Natural Bridge	1941–Present	Engine 24	Former Station 53
25	1600 North 16th	1885–1953	Engine 25, District Chief 4, Hose Wagon 4 (1942–1953)—Last station with horse-drawn apparatus; last run, March 25, 1927	Razed
5–25	2123 North Market	1953–1971	Engine 5, Engine 25, Hook & Ladder 2, Hose Wagon 4 (All units 1953–1971)	Became Station 5
26	2100 North 2nd	1887–1942	Engine 26	Commercial Business
26	4520 Margaretta	1942–Present	Engine 26, Hook & Ladder 21 (1942–1975), Hook & Ladder 9 (1975–1986), Medic 12 (2000–2014), Medic 26 (2014–Present)	Former Station 54
27	4571 Easton	1888–1932	Engine 27—While being razed on July 17, 1985, building collapsed resulting in 2-alarm-plus response with one fatality.	Former Chemical 4 and Chemical 5
43–27	4810 Enright	1932–1942	Engine 27, Engine 43, and Hook & Ladder 15 (All 1932–1942), Inhalator 3 (1933–1942), Gasoline Supply Truck 2	Became Station 28
27	5435 Partridge	1942–Present	Engine 27 (1942–2011), Hook & Ladder 20 (1942–1975), Hook & Ladder 7, (1975–1986), Marine 4, Truck 27 (2011–Present)	Former Station 55
28	3934 Morgan (became Enright)	1888–1960	Engine 28, Hook & Ladder 9 (1893–1960), USC–Salvage 3 (1920)	Former Chemical 4
28	3934 Enright (formerly Morgan)	1961–1965	Engine 28, Hook & Ladder 9	Private Residence
28	4810 Enright	1975–Present	Engine 28, Hook & Ladder 15 (1975–2009), Hook & Ladder 5 (2009–Present), Battalion Chief 5, HazMat Task Force	Former Station 43–27
29	1219 Old Manchester*	1888–1965	Engine 29 *Later became South Vandeventer	Business/Office Space
21–29	200 South Vandeventer	1965–1978	Engine 21, Engine 29, Hook & Ladder 5 (1965–1972), Rescue 1 (1965–1966), Hose Wagon 12 (1966–1971), Battalion Chief 7 (1965–?)	Became Station 29
29	200 South Vandeventer	1978–Present	Engine 29 (1978–2011), Snorkel 2 (1972–1975), Snorkel 5 (1975–1986), Foam 3 (1992–1994), Foam 4 (1994–2004), Rescue 2 (1986–Present), Medic 29 (2000–2011), HazMat 3, Truck 29 (2011–2018), Engine 29 (2018–Present)	Former Station 21–29 In Service
30	5524 Vernon	1892–1957	Engine 30	Razed
30	541 DeBaliviere	1957–Present	Engine 30 (1957–2011), Truck 30 (2011–Present)	In Service
31	3945 Kossuth	1892–1953	Engine 31, District Chief 11 (1907)	Razed
31	4408 Donovan	1953–Present	Engine 31, Hose Wagon 9 (1958–1960), Hook & Ladder 4 (1969–1971), Medic 31 (1999–Present)	In Service
32	2000 Washington	1892–1919	Engine 32, Hook & Ladder 8, Fuel Wagon 8, Chemical 4 (1892–1896), Water Tower 2 (1896), Fuel Wagon 2 (1902–1919)	Became Repair Shop Present Day–Cider Bar
32	503 North 20th	1919–1971	Engine 32, Hook & Ladder 8	Private Residence
7–32	2600 LaSalle	1971–1974	Engine 7, Engine 32, Hook & Ladder 8 (Aerialscope 8)	Became Station 7
32	3500 South Grand	1975–Present	Engine 32, Engine 33 (1975–1976), Hook & Ladder 14 (1976–1986), Medic 32 (1999–Present)	Former Station 38
33	3324 Park	1895–1975	Engine 33 (1895–1963), Hose Wagon 8 (1942–1949), Engine 21 (1963–1965), Hook & Ladder 5 (1963–1965), Engine 33 (1965–1975)	Razed
33	8300 North Broadway (New)	1976–Present	Engine 33 (1976–2011), Medic 33 (1999–Present), Truck 33 (2011–2020), Engine 33 (2020)	Former Station 37
34	8227 South Broadway	1895–Present	Engine 34 (1895–2011), Truck 34 (2011–Present)	In Service
35	5450 Arsenal	1895–Present	Engine 35 (1895–2011), Hook & Ladder 10 (1895–1986), Battalion Chief 803, Medic 35 (1999–Present), Truck 35 (2011–Present) Fuel Wagon 9	Remodeled 1959-1960 In Service
36	1719 North Union (Orig.)	1897–1910	Engine 36—All-wood structure (first of only two such); no known photograph	Razed
36	1719 North Union (New)	1911–1942	Engine 36 (First motorized apparatus, 1910 Webb 700-GPM pumper, assigned here)	Privately Owned
36	5000 South Kingshighway	1942–Present	Engine 36 (1942–2011), Hook & Ladder 23 (1942–1975), Hook & Ladder 4 (1975–2012), Truck 36 (2011–Present), Hook & Ladder 3 (2012–Present)	Former Station 56

PAID STATIONS

Station	Address	Dates Occupied	Occupied By	Former/Became
37	8300 North Broadway (Orig.)	1897–1909	Engine 37—All-wood structure (second of only two such)	Became Station 33
37	8300 North Broadway (New)	1909–1976	Engine 37 (1909–1976), Hook & Ladder 3 (1932–1976)	Became Station 33
38	3500 South Grand	1899–1975	Engine 38 (1899–1976), Hook & Ladder 16 (1905–1942), Inhalator 2 (1933–1942), Gas Truck 4 (1935–1955), Hose Wagon 6 (1942–1971), Gas Truck 2 (1955–19XX)	Became Station 32
40–41	707 North 11th	1904–1956	Engine 40, Engine 41, Hook & Ladder 13 (All 1904–1956), Hose Wagon 2 (1928–1942), Inhalator 1 (1933–1942), Engine 18 (1941–1942), Hose Wagon 1 (1942–1956)	Business/Office Space
40–41	921 Delmar	1956–1975	Engine 40, Engine 41, Hook & Ladder 13 (All 1956–1975), Hose Wagon 1 (1956–1973), Battalion Chief 1	Razed
42	5747 Manchester (MO Hwy. 100)	1905–1975	Engine 42 (1905–1975), Hook & Ladder 18 (1957–1958), Hook & Ladder 10 (1959–1960)	Became Station 6
43	723 North Kingshighway	1905–1932	Engine 43, Hook & Ladder 15, Fuel Wagon 10	Razed
43–27	4810 Enright	1932–1942	Engine 27, Engine 43, and Hook & Ladder 15 (All 1932–1942), Inhalator 3 (1933–1942), Gasoline Supply Truck 2	Became Station 43
43	4810 Enright	1942–1975	Engine 43 and Hook & Ladder 15, Hose Wagon 10 (1942–1946), Hose Wagon 12 (1949–1966), Battalion Chief 9, Rescue Squad (1966–1974), Battalion Chief 5	Became Station 28
44	4425 South Compton	1906–1942	Engine Company 44	Became Station 4
45	914 Allen	1906–1939	Engine 45	Private Residence
46	4161 Kennerly	1908–1942	Engine 46	Became Station 10
47	5214 West Florissant	1909–1942	Engine 47	Became Station 12
48	1400 Shawmut	1909–1942	Engine 48 (1909–1942), Hook & Ladder 17 (1909–1942)	Became Station 13
49	3523 Magnolia	1909–1942	Engine 49	Became Station 14
50	223 South Newstead	1913–1942	Engine 50 (1913–1942), Hook & Ladder 19 (1913–1942)	Became Station 18
51	4300 Eichelberger	1910–1942	Engine 51 (1910–1942) Last station built for horses	Became Station 19
52	6810 Clayton	1911–1942	Engine 52 (1911–1942), Hook & Ladder 18	Became Station 22
53	5245 Natural Bridge	1922–1942	Engine 53	Became Station 24
54	4520 Margaretta	1917–1942	Engine 54 and Hook & Ladder 21 (1917–1942), Inhalator 4 (1933–1942)	Became Station 26
55	5435 Partridge	1922–1942	Engine 55 and Hook & Ladder 20 (Both units 1922–1942)	Became Station 27
56	5000 South Kingshighway	1926–1942	Engine 56 and Hook & Ladder 23 (Both units 1926–1942)	Became Station 36

MISCELLANEOUS FACILITIES

Facility	Address	Dates Occupied	Occupied By	Former/Became
Repair Shop	508 North 3rd	1885–1902	Repair shop believed to be in basement of Station 23	Razed
Repair Shop	2004 Washington	1902–1919	Repair shop adjacent to Station 32	Razed
Repair Shop	2000–2004 Washington	1919–1929	Repair shop, formerly Fire Station 32	Partially Razed—Remaining Cider Bar
Repair Shop	1125 Spruce	1929–200X	Behind Station 14–24 (when new) and now Station 2. Operated until mid-2000s when services farmed out to Metro.	In service for storage
Repair Shop	3300 Spruce	200X–2018	Metro Bus Central Facility—Fire apparatus repairs contracted to Metro Bus, mid-2000s–2018	Contract terminated
Repair Shop	1200 Central Industrial	2018–Present	Shared facility with St. Louis Refuse	In service
Warehouse	2400 North 22nd	18XX–1953	Between Fire Station 5 and horse hospital	Razed
Warehouse	3601 Goodfellow	2000s	Storage facility for apparatus and equipment	Vacated
Horse Hospital	2408 North 22nd	1874–19XX	Adjacent to warehouse between it and Fire Station 5	Razed
Training School	1125 Spruce	1929–1990	Behind Station 14–24 (when new) and now Station 2. Operated until Dec. 27, 1988, when training moved to new headquarters.	In service for storage
Training School	1421 North Jefferson	1990–Present	Former Jefferson–Cass Health Center, originally constructed in 1958. Remodeled for headquarters in late 1980s.	In service
Fire Alarm	4971 Oakland Avenue	1964–1990	Fire Alarm	City Owned
Fire Alarm	1421 North Jefferson	1990–Present	Fire Alarm	In Service
Fire Alarm Warehouse	2400 North 22nd	1953–19XX	Fire Alarm Warehouse	Former Fire Station 5
Fire Alarm Warehouse	212 South Vandeventer	19XX–198X	Fire Alarm Warehouse (Next to Station 21–29)	Razed
Headquarters	1421 North Jefferson	1990–Present	Former Jefferson–Cass Health Center, originally constructed in 1958. Remodeled for headquarters in late 1980s.	In service
EMS Headquarters	2634 Hampton	1997–Present	Former St. Louis Police Department 2nd Precinct, originally built in 1936.	In service

LAMBERT–ST LOUIS INTERNATIONAL AIRPORT/NOW ST. LOUIS LAMBERT INTERNATIONAL AIRPORT FIRE STATIONS				
Facility	Address	Dates Occupied	Occupied By	Former/Became
CFR Station	Lambert Airport	1958–1963	CFR Station that was Missouri Air National Guard Hangar 1	
CFR Station	Lambert Airport	1963–Present	Only CFR Station, 1963–1984. Closed in 200X and presently used for storage.	
Main ARFF Station	6171 Aviation Drive	1984–Present	Main ARFF Station and Administrative Offices	
West ARFF Station	4640 Fee Fee	2005–Present	West ARFF Station	

ST. LOUIS WORLD'S FAIR FIRE STATIONS—1904				
Facility	Address	Dates Occupied	Occupied By	Former/Became
Fire Station 1	Forest Park	1903–1905	Storage for hand-drawn apparatus	
Fire Station 2	Forest Park	1903–1905	Storage for hand-drawn apparatus	
Fire Station 3	Forest Park	1903–1905	Storage for hand-drawn apparatus	
Fire Station 4	Forest Park	1903–1905	Engine 42, Chemical Company 1, Hook & Ladder 14. Only staffed World's Fair Fire Station.	Razed, 1905

UNDERWRITERS SALVAGE CORPS				
Facility	Address	Dates Occupied	Occupied By	Former/Became
Salvage House 1	711 Locust	1884–1903	Salvage 1	Razed
Salvage House 1	1127 Locust	1903–1918	Salvage 1	Razed
Salvage House 1	1211 Pine	1918–1947	Salvage 1 (1918–1947), Salvage 2 (1938–1947), Salvage 3 (1938–1947)	Razed
Salvage House 2	1310 Merchant	1887–1916	Salvage 2	Razed
Salvage House 2	2310 Sidney	1916–1938	Salvage 2. Company moved to Station 1 in 1938. Later became O. T. Hodge Chile Company Parlor.	Razed
Salvage House 3	3321 Locust	1893–1938	Salvage 3. Company moved to Station 1 in 1938.	Closed 1938–1941
Salvage House 3	3321 Locust	1941–1955	Salvage 3. Later became private residence.	Private Residence

There are possible discrepancies with the information provided herein. Where corrections or additions are available, please contact Robert Pauly at paulyr@stlouis-mo.gov or Dennis Maag at fireapparatusfan@swbell.net.

EPILOGUE

Fire stations are something that most people in the community really don't think much about. True, they house the emergency apparatus that will respond during their greatest time of need and provide shelter to the firefighters who lay in wait. But how often do people really consider the buildings themselves? Looking at the stations that presently serve the citizens of St. Louis is really taking a step back in history. Of the thirty stations currently operating in the city, more than a third are over a hundred years old with the newest station built over forty-five years ago! This in itself is a feat and truly a testament to those before us who oversaw the construction of these stations as well as all of those who ensure that they continue to be functional today. While these stations outwardly appear the same as when new, many subtle changes have been made to allow them to continue to be used safely and efficiently today. Early motorized apparatus were only six to seven feet wide and around twenty feet long and weighed less than 15,000 pounds. As more equipment and water was carried and aerial ladders were mounted on top of apparatus, the vehicles got heavier, wider, and taller. Today, most vehicles are more than eight feet wide, and some aerial apparatus are nearly twelve feet tall, fifty feet long, and weigh 80,000 pounds! Building new stations in landlocked areas during cash-strapped times is cost prohibitive. So in order to implement the Total Quint Concept, funding from a 1986 bond issue was used to reinforce floors and widen and heighten bay doors to accommodate aerial-equipped apparatus. Modern amenities often taken for granted such as kitchens, sleeping areas, heating and cooling, plumbing, electrical, and computer systems have required modernization. Funding from a 1998 bond issue allowed significant renovations to living quarters in many stations from 2001 to 2006.

The following photos show a present-day view of the stations. The St. Louis Fire Department has done a wonderful job of making needed changes to these buildings—some of which are more than a hundred years old—while maintaining their historic character. Comparing these contemporary photos to those shown earlier in the book will provide a glimpse of these changes. The front of some stations have a different look, with taller door openings, modern bay doors, and updated station numbers. The side of the stations show the ductwork and exhaust extraction systems, as well as windows bricked in to improve efficiency for heating and cooling. The roofs reveal kitchen vents, HVAC systems, and the various antennas for modern radio and computer equipment. A view of the outside shows nearly every station with a locked, fenced lot for the protection of personal vehicles, perhaps a sad statement of the times.

Join me as we continue our journey that started back in the early 1800s and finishes today. From their outward architectural characteristics to their interiors—many of which proudly display photos of fires, firefighters, and apparatus of the past—the beauty and character of St. Louis fire stations have not changed. Much like the old stone foundation seen in the photo of Station 34, built in 1895, the members and their stations are the foundation of the St. Louis Fire Department. These stations hold the memory of those bygone days, while the firefighters maintain their traditions for generations to come and give them the right to refer to themselves as *Justifiably Proud!*

—Dennis J. Maag

STATIONS TODAY

FIRE STATION 1

2910 South Jefferson Avenue

While the general appearance of Fire Station 1 has remained the same since it opened in 1975, the signage above the doors better reflects the companies assigned there today, including Engine 1, Rescue Squad 1, the Collapse Rescue Task Force, and STARRS USAR unit. Those apparatus have grown in size as well as the equipment carried as is evidenced by the photo of Rescue Squad 1, a 2017 Spartan/SVI, when compared to that shown on page 91 from the 1960s.

FIRE STATION 2

312 Tucker Boulevard

The appearance of Station 2 has not changed much since the modifications made in 1966. When viewing from the rear, the training school and repair shop no longer operate here, but the fire department wrecker, air unit, and command post are still stationed here.

FIRE STATION 4

4425 South Compton Avenue

Fire Station 4 outwardly appears like it did when it opened in 1906. This view shows that some of the windows have been bricked in, presumably to ease the work of the HVAC system. It's interesting to note that there is a bench in front of the station just like there was in the photo taken in the 1960s on page 92. Today, Truck 4 and Battalion Chief 804 are assigned here.

Truck 4 operates this 2017 Spartan/ Smeal 75-foot quint.

FIRE STATION 5

2123 North Market Street

While Station 5 appears much the same as when new in 1953, the landscape of the neighborhood has changed dramatically with a great reduction in residential buildings, many actually burned out. Located near the site of the new headquarters of the National Geospatial Intelligence Agency that's currently under construction, it's home to Truck 5, Hook and Ladder 1, Medic 5, and Battalion Chief 801.

FIRE STATION 6

5747 Manchester Avenue

Station 6's appearance remains much the same as the photo on page 94, but the firefighters have cleaned up and painted the signage over the door, placing a large "6" over the "42" to reflect the current assignment of Engine Company 6.

FIRE STATION 7

2600 LaSalle Street

When new in 1975, Station 7 was home to Engines 7 and 32 as well as Hook and Ladder 18. Over the years, reductions in staff and companies have led to Truck 7 being the only fire company assigned here, along with the Fire Investigative unit.

The City of St. Louis Unified Command Unit is also stored at Station 7. It is a 2012 International/LDV that is used by multiple agencies in the event of a major event or disaster.

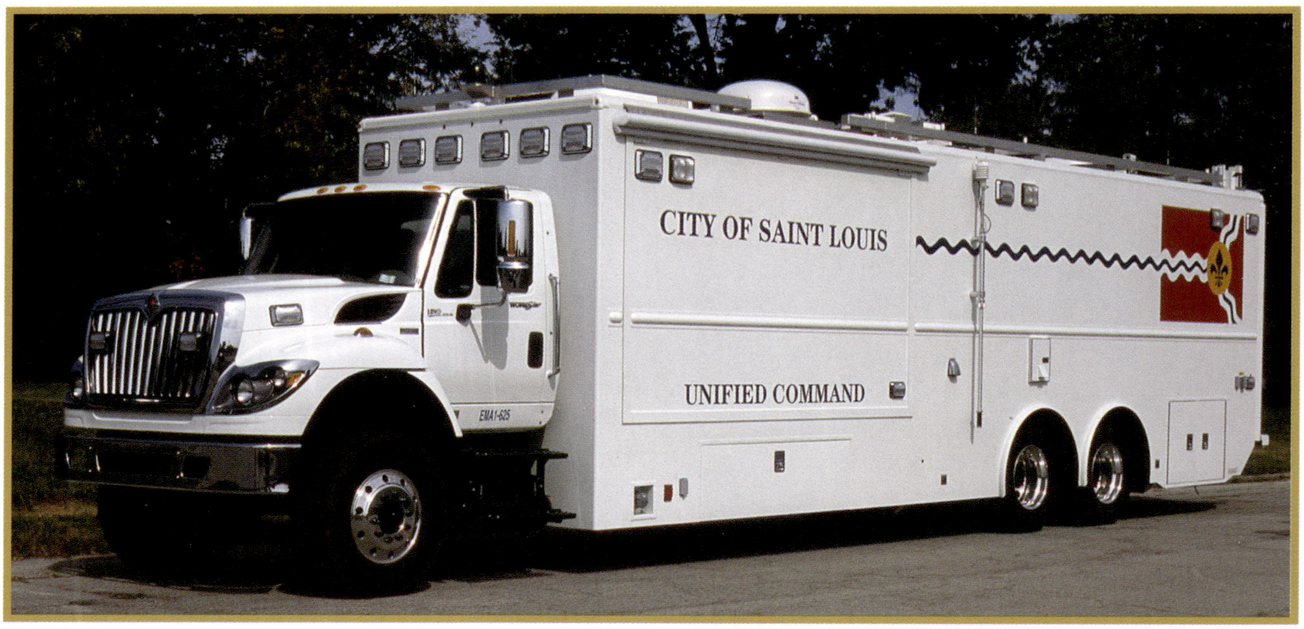

FIRE STATION 8

1501 Salisbury Street

Station 8 is one of the most beautiful stations operated by the St. Louis Fire Department. A close look at the front of the building and the ramp, when compared to the photo on page 95, shows how the driveway and floor were lowered to accommodate an aerial-equipped apparatus.

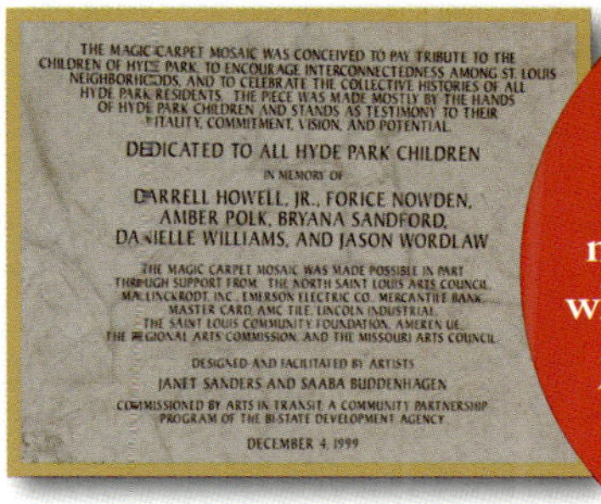

The dedication on the wall and the mural on the sidewalk are in memory of the six children who perished in an arson fire just across the street from the 8's on March 12, 1999.

FIRE STATION 9

814 La Beaume Street

With the exception of new bay doors, windows, and larger trees surrounding it, Fire Station 9 appears much as it did when opened in 1957.

FIRE STATION 10

4161 Kennerly Avenue

Station 10 appears much the same as it did in the photo on page 97, except for the addition of the exhaust for the diesel extraction system and the recycle bin outside the station. The crew of Truck 10 poses proudly with their 2017 Spartan/Smeal 75-foot quint.

FIRE STATION 11

2224 South Seventh Street

When Station 11 opened in 1963, Engines 11 and 16, Hook and Ladder 1, and a foam truck were assigned here. Today, Truck 11 is the lone staffed company here, but it is home to the Marine Unit Task Force that is assigned a number of boats and support units for the team.

This 2012 Safe 27-foot boat is for fire and rescue responses on the Mississippi River.

FIRE STATION 12

5214 West Florissant Avenue

Station 12 may appear the same as the photo on page 98, but a closer look shows that some of the framing and a window above the bay door under the arch have been removed to accommodate today's larger apparatus. Hook and Ladder 6 is the only unit assigned here with a 2009 Spartan/Smeal 125-foot 1250–GPM quint.

FIRE STATION 13

1400 Shawmut Place

Station 13 retains the same ornate beauty and magnificence on the front of the station as it did when it opened as Station 48 in 1909, and is the only station to still have metal tracks in the bay floor where the horse-drawn steamer would park. Featuring an updated bay door and windows, it's interesting to note than many of the windows on the side of the building have been bricked in. Station 13 was one of several stations that had a spiral staircase installed that led from the apparatus floor to the captain's room on the second floor during the remodels in the 1980s, and still has five poles in the bay.

FIRE STATION 14

3523 Magnolia Avenue

Station 14 features updated windows and a new bay door. The bench out front is a longtime staple in front of many St. Louis fire stations.

This rear view of Station 14 shows the ductwork for the exhaust extraction system. You can also see the bricked-in opening on the second floor that was likely where hay was hoisted into the station during the horse-drawn days.

Note the address on the mail slot.

FIRE STATION 17

3238 Martin Luther King Drive

The photo on the right shows the opposite side of Station 17 compared to the view on page 101. In the photo above, note the side bay door that once accessed a garage when District Chief 6 was assigned here.

FIRE STATION 19

6624 Morgan Ford Road

The simple beauty of Station 19, located on the corner of Morgan Ford and Haven, continues to blend in well with the Boulevard Heights neighborhood, much as it did when it first opened in 1956. It's as much of a landmark to local residents as the Haven pub across the street.

FIRE STATION 20

5600 Prescott Avenue

When Station 20 opened in 1960, it was home to Engine 20, Hook and Ladder 12, and Hose Wagon 7. Today, Truck 20 and Battalion Chief 806 call it home. Note the Dalmatian above the bay door and "RET" above H&L 12.

FIRE STATION 22

1229 McCausland Avenue

When new, Station 22 was home to a pumper, a hook and ladder, and a hose wagon. While Truck 22 is the only staffed unit today, a number of apparatus are also stored here including Former Reserve Engine 5's 1977 Duplex/Howe pumper, the only one to have been painted red by St. Louis.

FIRE STATION 23

6500 Michigan Avenue

Station 23 appears much as it did when it opened in 1921, including the roman numerals above the bay door. When looking at the size of the station and how tight it is for Engine 23 and Medic 23, it's amazing that it once housed a pumper, a hook and ladder, a fuel wagon, and a district chief in that same small space!

FIRE STATION 24

5245 Natural Bridge Avenue

This photo of Station 24 shows the addition of the diesel exhaust extraction system and a nice view of the hose tower.

Engine 24's crew proudly posing in front of their 2010 Spartan/Smeal 2000–GPM pumper.

FIRE STATION 26

4520 Margaretta Avenue

Housing Engine 26 and Medic 26, Station 26 appears much the same as it did when it opened as Station 54 in 1917. Note the framed addition cantilevered on the left side of the building. It's not known what it was originally designed for, but after an interior remodel it's now used for a locker room.

The original dedication plate when the station was built as Station 55

FIRE STATION 27

5435 Partridge Avenue

When you compare the above photo of Station 27 to the image on page 107, you'll notice that the bay door has been heightened to permit modern aerial-equipped apparatus. Also note the addition of the "27" above the front bay door.

The 27's 2001 Spartan/Smeal 2000–GPM 75-foot quint

FIRE STATION 28

4810 Enright Avenue

This has always been a busy station for the St. Louis Fire Department, and the companies currently assigned here—Engine 28, Hook and Ladder 5, and the HazMat Task Force—remain very active today. Many St. Louis stations have personalized items around their station, but this may be the only one with banana trees!

FIRE STATION 29

200 South Vandeventer Avenue

With the exception of newer bay doors, Station 29 appears for the most part the same as it did when it opened as the 21's in 1965 and was home to Engine 21, Engine 29, Hook and Ladder 5, Rescue Squad 1, and Battalion Chief 7. Today, Engine 29 and Rescue Squad 2, respond from here along with HazMat 3 as shown here.

Dedication plaque and HazMat 3 2009 International/ Hackney

FIRE STATION 30

541 DeBaliviere Avenue

In 2012, Engine Company 30 celebrated 120 years of service to the St. Louis Fire Department. At that time, members noted this milestone below the Fire Station 30 signage.

STATION 31

4408 Donovan Avenue

Protecting the St. Louis Hills neighborhood since 1953, Station 31 looks much as it did when new. Today, Engine 31 and Medic 31 call the station at 4408 Donovan home. Note the original dedication.

STATION 32

3500 South Grand Boulevard

Station 32 has maintained much of the original character it had when it opened in 1899 as Station 38. Members have painted a "2" over the "8" to represent Engine House 32. Note the dormer above the second floor that leads into the attic space.

STATION 33

8300 North Broadway

Fire Station 33 still bears "Engine House No. 37" in the brickwork at the top of the building. However, members of have attempted to turn the numbering in the shield above the bay door into a "33." Note the locked, fenced gate to the left of the station protecting the members' personal vehicles.

FIRE STATION 34

8227 South Broadway

With the exception of some of the windows being bricked in, an updated bay door, and some exterior lighting, Station 34 looks for the most part the way it did when it was built in 1895. When viewing the side and rear of the structure, it's interesting to note the stones that were placed as a foundation to keep the rear of the station level with the street at the front.

STATION 35

5450 Arsenal Street

Home to Truck 35 and Medic 35, Station 35 appears on the outside much the same as it did after the remodeling in 1960. The addition on the rear of the building with the small garage door is presently occupied by Battalion Chief 803.

FIRE STATION 36

5000 South Kingshighway Boulevard

Probably my favorite station in all of St. Louis due to its beauty and the setting at the wedge of Kingshighway and Christy. It retains most of the original character from 1926, but a close look at the front of the building shows that the arched opening above the bay door was widened and the height increased to accommodate the larger modern aerial apparatus. The modification was tastefully completed, and if you didn't know how the original building looked, you would not likely be able to tell the difference. A walk around the building shows beautiful lines in the construction no matter what side you are on.

ST. LOUIS FIRE DEPARTMENT HEADQUARTERS

1421 North Jefferson Avenue

The present location of St. Louis Fire Department Headquarters was originally built in 1958–1959 and opened as the Jefferson–Cass Health Center serving residents of the Pruitt-Igoe housing complex. In the late 1980s, the building was renovated to serve as the St. Louis Fire Department Headquarters, which opened in 1990. Also located here is the training academy, drill tower, and dispatching for both fire and EMS. The building is on the National Register of Historic Places due to the role it played as a health center during the 1960s.

ST. LOUIS FIRE DEPARTMENT EMS HEADQUARTERS

2634 Hampton Avenue

This building located at 2634 Hampton currently serves as the St. Louis Fire Department EMS Headquarters. Originally built in 1936 for the St. Louis Police Department Second District, it reflects what may be considered the Streamline Moderne characteristics of the Art Deco period. The St. Louis Fire Department opened the facility for EMS Headquarters in 1997.

ST. LOUIS–LAMBERT INTERNATIONAL AIRPORT MAIN STATION

6171 Aviation Drive

The St. Louis Fire Department operates from two stations at St. Louis–Lambert International Airport. The main station located at 6171 Aviation Drive opened in 1984 and houses the administrative offices for the ARFF operation and features five drive-through bays.

ST. LOUIS–LAMBERT INTERNATIONAL AIRPORT WEST STATION

4640 Fee Fee Road

The west station at Lambert is located at 4640 Fee Fee Road and opened in 2005. This facility has three bays and houses a variety of apparatus.

Unit 53 is a 2005 Ford stairway unit.

THE SURVIVORS

FIRE STATION 1
2411 McNair Avenue
Operated from 1874 to 1971

FIRE STATION 3
3648 South Broadway
Operated from 1919 to 1969

FIRE STATION 7
1304 South Eighteenth Street
Operated from 1897 to 1975

FIRE STATION 26
2100 North Second Street
Operated from 1887 to 1952

FIRE STATION 28
3934 Enright Avenue
Operated from 1961 to 1965

FIRE STATION 29
1219 South Vandeventer (formerly Old Manchester)
Operated from 1888 to 1965

FORMER ST. LOUIS FIRE STATIONS

FIRE STATION 32
2000 Washington Avenue
Operated from 1892 to 1919 as Station 32 and 1919 to 1929 as the repair shop

FIRE STATION 32
503 North Twentieth Street
Operated from 1919 to 1971

FIRE STATION 36
1719 North Union Boulevard
Operated from 1897 to 1942

FIRE STATION 40 & 41
707 North Eleventh Street
Operated from 1904 to 1956

Photo by Dave Dubowski

FIRE STATION 45
914 Allen Avenue
Operated from 1906 to 1939

UNDERWRITERS SALVAGE CORPS STATION 3
3321 Locust Street
Operated from 1918 to 1955

INDEX